Populuxe

Alfred A. Knopf   New York   1987

Populuxe

Thomas Hine

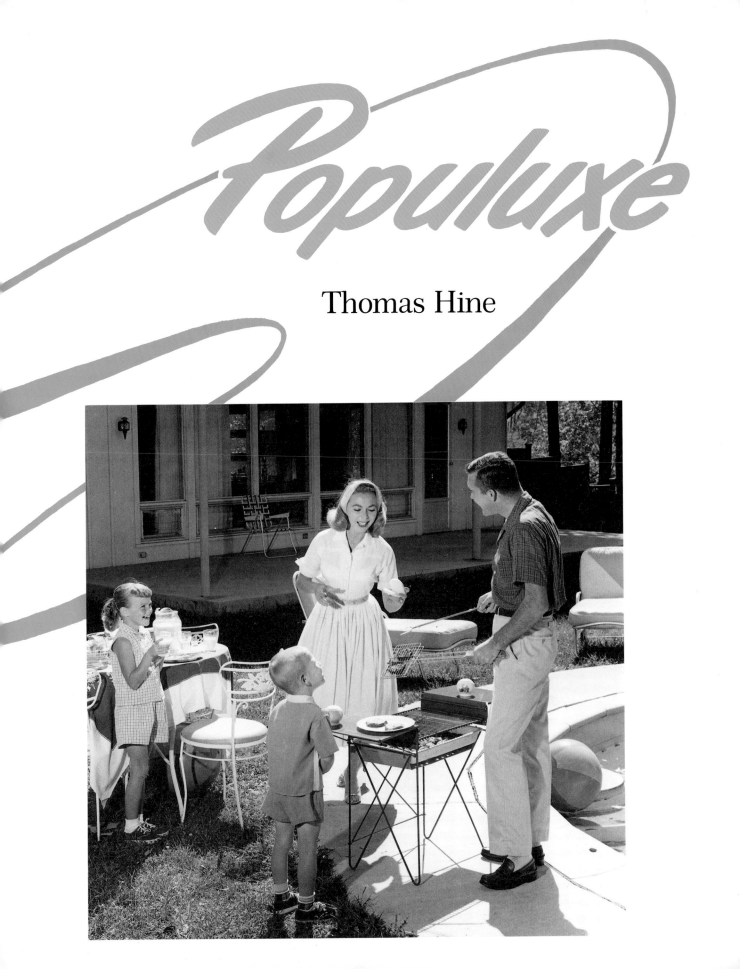

This Is a Borzoi Book
Published by Alfred A. Knopf, Inc.

Grateful acknowledgment is made to Schroder Music Company
for permission to reprint an excerpt from the song "Little
Boxes," words and music by Malvina Reynolds. © Schroder
Music Company (ASCAP). Used by permission. All rights reserved.

Library of Congress Cataloging-in-Publication Data
Hine, Thomas
Populuxe.
Includes index.
1. Design—United States—History—20th century.
2. Design, Industrial—United States—History—20th
century. 3. United States—Popular culture. I. Title.
NK1404.H54   1986   745.4'4973   86-45270
ISBN 0-394-54593-1   0-394-74014-9 (pbk.)

First Edition, November 18, 1986.
First Paperback Edition, November 1987.

Manufactured in Japan

To my mother and my sister Genevieve.
We tried to be a Populuxe family.

Contents

Populuxe

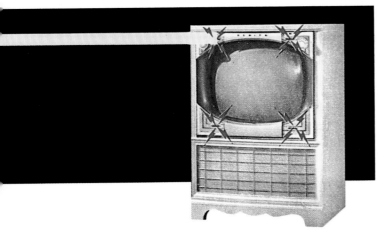

Taking Off

The decade from 1954 to 1964 was one of history's great shopping sprees, as many Americans went on a baroque bender and adorned their mass-produced houses, furniture and machines with accouterments of the space age and of the American frontier. "Live your dreams and meet your budget," one advertisement promised, and unprecedented numbers of Americans were able to do it. What they bought was rarely fine, but it was often fun. There were so many things to buy—a power lawn mower, a modern dinette set, a washer with a window through which you could see the wash water turn disgustingly gray, a family room, a charcoal grill. Products were available in a lurid rainbow of colors and a steadily changing array of styles. Commonplace objects took extraordinary form, and the novel and exotic quickly turned commonplace.

It was, materially, a kind of golden age, but it was one that left few monuments because the pleasures of its newfound prosperity were, like Groucho Marx's secret word, "something you find around the house." There was so much wealth it did not need to be shared. Each householder was able to have his own little Versailles along a cul-de-sac. People were physically separated, out on their own in a new muddy and unfinished landscape, but they were also linked as never before through advertising, television and magazines. Industry saw them as something new, "a mass market," an overwhelmingly powerful generator of profits and economic growth. There was ebullience in this grand display of appetite, a naïveté that was winning and, today, touching.

Populuxe is about the material objects of this highly materialistic age. Things were not only more common and more available than before, they were also invested with greater meaning. It is a look at the objects and the society in which they were meant to fit. It is an interpretation of a crucial moment in American history, one which determined the environment in which we live today, but many of whose attitudes seem distant, enigmatic and even quaint.

Populuxe does not consist of a single look. It is more an attitude expressed by a family of looks, a series of options added to such utilitarian objects as a Levitt house or a bottom-of-the-line Plymouth. It speaks of optimism and opulence and encompasses such tendencies as "swept-wing styling" and "the Forward Look," automobile company slogans that expressed the speed, the motion, the fantasy available in a De Soto Fireflite or an Olds Rocket 88. It encompasses "sheer" appliances, whose flat, right-angled lines were intended to make kitchens feel as clean and efficient as scientists' laboratories or jet planes.

As in most periods, mass tastes during the postwar years were often at odds with what was considered to be good taste, or educated taste. People who owned Studebakers and voted for Stevenson felt superior to those who voted for Eisenhower and bought Chevy Bel Airs. Today, the ideological difference between the Raymond Loewy Studebaker and the two-toned, tailfinned Chevy appears insignificant. What stands out is that there was so tremendous a number of people with the ability to buy so many things and leave such a significant material record of their fantasies and aspirations. During the Populuxe decade, the objects people could buy took on a special exaggerated quality. They celebrate confidence in the future, the excitement of the present, the sheer joy of having so much. Today we are inclined to marvel at the naïveté of the period or feel nausea at its overindulgence. Still, we cannot help seeing it all around us. It has made its way into contemporary art, into New Wave style, into restaurants and rock videos and even into antique stores. This re-examination of our recent past began behind a shield of irony, but by now we are ready to admit that much of what was made in that time is worth looking at, and some was even beautiful.

The essence of Populuxe is not merely having things. It is having things in a way that they'd never been had before, and it is an expression of outright, thoroughly vulgar joy in being able to live so well. "You will have a greater chance to be yourself than any people in the history of civilization," *House Beautiful* told its readers in 1953. The magazine went on to say that the greatness of America would be expressed by enrichment of the environment, and by the addition of new equipment to the household, and by giving up European models and, instead, finding inspiration in the American past and, most of all, in its promising future.

Populuxe means heavy pieces of living-room furniture standing on little

Barbie and Ken c., 1960. When you bought them they weren't wearing much, but plenty of clothes were available separately.

spindly legs, in an effort to achieve "a striking contemporary look." And it means women balanced precariously on spike-heeled shoes trying to do precisely the same thing. But it also means wrought iron and dining-room sets with hutches instead of buffets. It means the rise of the tailfin and the overall heightening of the fantasy content of the automobile. It means ranch-style houses with "vanettes" in the bathroom and family room, lawns and backyard barbecues, and it means Cape Cod houses with all those same features. It means pink washing machines with push-button panels and portable air conditioners and dishwashers. In essence, Populuxe is a way of referring to the moment when America found a way of turning out fantasy on an assembly line. Color and styling were applied to objects that had always been viewed as purely practical. The advertising industry was able to associate goods with moods, and many consumers fell into a pattern of buying a car, or even a stove, not because the old one was worn out, but simply because they felt like it.

The symbolic queen of Populuxe was Barbie, a doll who made her debut in 1959. She was an 11½-inch late adolescent, whose 3¼–3–4¾ measurements caused a certain consternation at first. Dolls didn't have figures then. But the suggestion of breasts were to be the least of it. The low price tag for the doll itself was primarily a come-on to lure the prepubescent doll owner into a flurry of anticipatory consumption. In true Populuxe fashion, Barbie was important not for herself but for all that could be added to her. She had party dresses, and gowns for the prom, and a wedding ensemble, casual clothes, outdoor clothes and outfits for many professions and avocations. She had a boyfriend, Ken, a little sister, Skipper, and assorted friends. She had a split-level house, a beauty parlor and a Corvette. There was always something new to buy for her—a more stylish outfit, a new kind of fashion, a different fantasy. She had a pillbox hat like the ones Jacqueline Kennedy wore; a little later she had a space suit. As with most of Populuxe, Barbie seemed only to be a product, but she turned out to be a way of life.

Populuxe is a synthetic word, created in the spirit of the many coined words of the time. Madison Avenue kept inventing words like "autodynamic," which described a shape of car which made no sense aerodynamically. Gardol was an invisible shield that stopped bullets and hard-hit baseballs to dramatize the effectiveness of a toothpaste. It was more a metaphor than an ingredient. Slenderella was a way to lose weight, and maybe meet a prince besides. Like these synthetic words, Populuxe has readily identifiable roots, and it reaches toward an ineffable emotion. It derives, of course, from populism and popularity, with just a fleeting allusion to pop art, which took Populuxe imagery and attitudes as subject matter. And it has luxury, popular luxury, luxury for all. This may be a contradiction in terms, but it is an expression of the spirit of the time and the rationale for many of the products that were produced. And, finally, Populuxe contains a thoroughly unnecessary "e," to give it class. That final embellishment of a practical and straightforward invention is what makes the word Populuxe, well, Populuxe.

It was not a candy-covered decade for all, of course. Black rural poverty was being transformed to black urban poverty. Integration was the great moral crusade of the time, and the reminder that many Americans were excluded from the benefits of a wealthy era presented a strong challenge to a society which was very proud of how many were included. But even here, integration was the desire of blacks to break into the American middle class, just as many other previously excluded groups had done. It had not yet turned into black power.

The decade's description of the average American probably fit very few of its citizens. It excluded not only blacks but residents of ethnic urban neighborhoods, the single, widowed and divorced and their children and a great many others who did not often show their faces in advertisements. Yet what was remarkable was not that many were excluded from the bounty of a prosperous time, but that a vast majority got a share of the wealth and were able to take large steps up the economic ladder.

In this time of great change people chose most often to celebrate change itself. "We are moving ahead," John Kennedy said repeatedly during his 1960 presidential campaign. "But we are not moving ahead rapidly enough." Forward motion at ever-increasing speed was what Americans expected from their

A colonial living room could co-exist with a modern kitchen, and no one would give it a second thought.

nation, their cars and their careers. Kennedy also promised "a New Frontier," which suggested that traditional American values and ideas would be able to serve the nation as it coped with the future. In this, he echoed the advertising of most of the previous decade, which embraced the rocket and the covered wagon with equal fervor, really as manifestations of the same spirit.

Television brought new faces into the living room, and sitcom families like the Nelsons became a new kind of neighbor.

The look of motion and efficient technology was balanced and mitigated by the look of togetherness, the imagery of early America and a nation that was founded, so one furniture advertisement put it, "by families like yours." Just as this period was obsessed with the future, it was also preoccupied with Americans' pioneering past in movies and television programs and furniture. Disneyland offered the choice between Frontierland and Tomorrowland. So did the American suburban house. The kitchen was futuristic, the dining room Early American. Nobody paid much attention to the inconsistency, any more than they gave a second thought to one of the characteristic materials of the time, "antique white" plastic, in which such products as radios, automatic drink mixers and party serving sets were available.

Many have seen this period of cultural upheaval as a long national snooze, in which the American public was apathetic and complacent. Indeed, there may have been a desire to let the traditional public concerns run on automatic pilot for a while, largely because so much was changing in people's private lives. Ike, fatherly and reassuring, seemed to be presiding as much on the golf course as in the White House. Senator Joseph McCarthy, and the fear of Communism he had so inflamed, suddenly disappeared in what seemed a puff of

acrid smoke. Korea was over too, a war that ended not in victory but in disengagement, and Americans found it easy to disengage their emotions from what happened there. There was amazingly little notice of the great migrations then under way—the emptying of the rural South and the black influx into northern cities, and the middle-class departure from the cities to the suburbs. These were experienced personally, not as a society.

Through it all, the residents of the world's mightiest nation seemed to be dozing on a hammock in the backyard, or seated in front of their television sets chuckling over the bland emergencies of the Andersons, the Stones, the Cleavers and other sitcom families. They were trying, they felt, to live peaceful, normal lives, reaping the blessings to which they were entitled as Americans.

Yet the normality to which they were trying to adhere was something entirely new—a way of life in which standards were set not by families and neighbors but by new kinds of authorities whose message came by television, magazines and the backs of boxes. This new life was being lived in a whole new kind of environment, a distended, sprawling metropolis that was, in Frank Lloyd Wright's phrase, everywhere and nowhere. The new suburbia was not picturesque and elitist, as earlier American suburbs had been. Rather it was a place where the scrape of the bulldozer shaped the land, and a newly massive middle class tried to figure out how to live. And the forms their blessings took—split-level houses with boomerang coffee tables, heavy turquoise-colored sinks standing precariously on slender metal rods and showy winged cars in the driveway—were bizarre, perhaps, but they felt right at the time.

Television changed the focus of the living room and gave rise to TV snacks, TV dinners, and other novel ways of eating.

The arrival of the television set made a big difference in people's lives. The moment it arrived, the household was transformed. The living-room furniture was rearranged so everyone could get a good view, and lives were planned around the TV schedule. It spawned the TV dinner and the TV tray. The TV screen was used even in print advertising to give the message increased authority. Most important, though, a new vision of modern life was available at the flick of a switch. There, on the screen, were Ozzie, Harriet, David "and the irrepressible Ricky," the perfect example of a family working together and solving their little problems. (A little later, Ricky became a rock singer, and Ozzie and Harriet were very supportive; they didn't yell "When are you going to stop that racket!" even once.) The extreme harmony of the Nelson family—mild bemusement was their strongest emotion—was too good to be true, but even though they were not always believable, television programs implicitly set standards. Many sat watching in new houses, in brand-new neighborhoods where only a year or two before farmers had harvested lettuce. They had taken on new obligations. They were paying new debts. Their careers were taking shapes that their parents might not have understood. The families on the sitcoms appeared to know what they were doing and take the world in stride; many of those watching were living lives of exhilarating disorientation.

Television was but one of their links to the new America. There was also the car, which by the middle of the decade had tailfins and sharp lines, and perhaps even a snazzy two-tone color scheme. And there were the magazines, dispensing information on the new life, along with advertisements for the products that would help people achieve it. Today, their luxuriously large, vividly colored pictures serve as a national family album that records a nation at a very formative stage.

Populuxe arose well after World War II, despite the orgy of consumption that characterized the immediate postwar years. The initial postwar period, from about 1946 to 1954, produced a lot of cars, a lot of babies, a lot of appliances, a lot of suburbs. Americans were catching up on the consumption they had put off during World War II and the Depression. This was the period when the unveiling of a model home in either the Long Island or the Pennsylvania Levittown could produce mile-long lines of would-be buyers, snaking through the muddy remains of farmers' fields. This first postwar boom produced record sales and consumption of many products that stood for decades.

But the primary aim of the immediate postwar era was to catch up. With the exception of the 1948 Cadillac, which had the first suggestion of tailfins, and a handful of other products, most of what was sold continued the streamlined locomotive and ocean-liner imagery of the prewar years. Or, as in the case of developments like the first two Levittowns, they were simple, massproduced responses to colossal demand. The immensely productive wartime economy was being transformed into the strongest consumer economy the world had ever seen. Americans were catching up with all that they had deferred and were even to buy some things they had only dreamed of. Getting the product on the market at a realistic price was the first priority.

The turning point came in 1954, an eventful year by any standard. It brought not only the downfall of McCarthy and the momentous Supreme Court decision outlawing segregated schools but also the introduction of sleek, powerful and finny low-priced cars and the emergence of a sexy, urgent new kind of popular music—rock and roll. Some 1.5 million new homes were built that year, the great majority of them outside the central cities; 1.4 million power lawn mowers were sold and 4 million babies were born. It was a year in which Americans began to feel less threatened by Communism, and more anxious to enjoy the fruits of American affluence. And it was also a year in which major corporations changed their marketing strategies in order to induce people to spend their increasing incomes.

The next decade—the Populuxe era—presented an invitation to indulge in the luxuries. To the simple mass-produced artifact that was known to be at the heart of every consumable, from salt shaker to house, was added an overlay of fantasy, of personalization, of style. Americans reveled in a kind of innocent

GOOD TASTE IS NEVER EXTREME

Certain people have it. Certain things, as well—that sense of right-ness we call good taste. You recognize it at once when it is there.

It is there in the '59 Plymouth, in the look, the lines of a car deliberately designed with flair, and with restraint. For good taste is neither stodgy nor bizarre. It is not conspicuous. Nor is it anony-mous. It does stand out, yes—but handsomely.

This year, so many people of good taste are responding to the car fashioned most particularly for them—the '59 Plymouth.

hedonism, buying objects in vibrant two-tone combinations of turquoise and taupe, charcoal and coral, canary and lime. Everything from a T-bird to a toaster took on a shape that made it seem to lean forward, ready to surge ahead. The highway and the kitchen filled up with objects whose lines were characterized by gentle curves coming to sharp points, in emulation of the exemplary object of the age—the jet fighter plane.

In automobiles, the change to the Populuxe attitude appeared with the introduction of the 1955 models and the beginning of the most frantic year of car buying America had yet experienced. Almost every make of American car suddenly took on lines that were angular and dynamic, and people bought. The event that truly signaled the arrival of Populuxe was the introduction of the 1955 Chevrolet. Its tailfins were quite modest, compared with what was to come later, but they were a strong contrast with the basic transportation image of previous years. It was, as people said at the time, a baby Cadillac, powerful, exciting, available in an array of lively color schemes. It was still a Chevy, and everyone knew that, but it allowed the Chevy buyer to partake fully of a moment when the act of breaking the sound barrier had taken on truly heroic qualities and rocketing into space was just around the corner. The Chevy buyer even had an edge over those who were buying more expensive, yet clearly more old-fashioned cars, such as Oldsmobiles and Chryslers—he was buying the future. The 1955 Chevrolet is a paradigm of Populuxe because it embodied the aspirations of the time and it was one of the most affordable automobiles of the era.

In their innards, Populuxe objects were deeply consistent. Their materials and engineering were dictated by the manufacturing process. People at the time seem to have understood that they were living with the benefits of the machine age, but unlike advocates of modern design, they saw no need to celebrate the industrial process. It was far more fun to let objects embody something many people felt, an almost limitless sense of possibility. Populuxe objects were symbols of achievement, affirmations that their owners had achieved a life of convenience and prosperity that their parents could only have dreamed of. Populuxe objects were frankly commercial. It was design intended solely to sell a product. What had previously been luxuries—automobiles, automatic washers, large front yards—were turning into necessities, but people still felt the need to celebrate and adorn them with features that at least suggested luxury.

Magazines like *House Beautiful* tried to set standards of acceptable consumption, but the prevailing spirit was distinctly nouveau riche. "Good taste is never extreme," proclaimed a 1959 Plymouth advertisement that showed a smartly dressed woman getting into a car whose massive tailfins make it almost a parody of the extremes of which the era was capable. People wanted to be known for their good taste, but they also wanted to have great showy things that demonstrated that they had arrived. Populuxe is vulgar by definition. It is the result of an unprecedented ability to acquire, reaching well down into the working class, to the sort of people who had historically been able to have only a few mean objects. These people did not acquire the good simple objects many tastemakers advocated. They had had it with simple, and now they wanted more.

People knew that what they were buying was mass-produced and synthetic, but few seemed to mind. Machine-made products were an improvement over the difficult, old-fashioned things that their parents and grandparents had used. And people also knew that they were purchasing a certain amount of sham. It wasn't much more than a little bit of chrome and some carpeting that turned a Ford Fairlane into a Galaxie, but a lot of people knowingly, and eagerly, paid the price. The manufacturers even sold this connection as a positive attribute. Only one year after Ford had made a big splash with its classic, two-seater Thunderbird, it ran an advertising campaign for its basic models which proclaimed that they were the only family cars "with Thunderbird styling." Admittedly, there was no acknowledgment that the Thunderbird shared at least a few of the characteristics of the basic Ford, but most people knew that. If you bought a Thunderbird, you were buying a full-strength fantasy. If your budget and needs ran to a lesser model, you could still partake of the T-bird dream by association.

Although Populuxe objects had a broad popular appeal, and could be found nearly everywhere, their overwrought design was primarily reserved for private

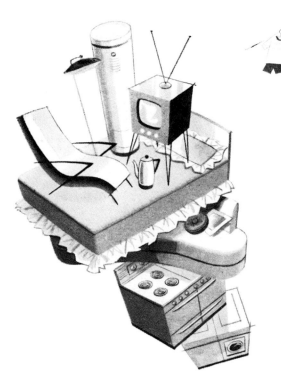

The Populuxe vision of prosperity and convenience encompassed a great number of objects, all styled to celebrate progress and dynamism, as in this chaise longue with tailfin arms.

indulgence, not public gestures. During the entire Populuxe era, the "official" style was European modernism, interpreted in a strict, rather ascetic way. While much of what Americans were buying was termed "modernistic," it was hardly modern in the way that tastemakers used that term. This led to a reversal of the age-old pattern in which seats of government and houses of worship received the highest craftsmanship and ornamentation a society could produce, while the individual house was relatively bare. During the Populuxe era, the town hall and even the church or synagogue might be a featureless glass-and-steel crate, while the individual home would be carefully landscaped and lavishly furnished with things that evoked different historical periods and the future besides. A few architects, notably Eero Saarinen and Edward Durrell Stone, caught the public imagination and contributed to the development of Populuxe design.

But for most design professionals, the Populuxe attitude bordered on the immoral. The Museum of Modern Art, for example, was an aggressive propagandist for European modernism and simplicity, and even some of the home and design magazines and mass magazines such as *Life* offered forums for those who warned Americans against ornamental overindulgence. They listened politely, then, like adolescents who have come into a windfall, went on a binge.

The Luckiest Generation

"Never before," *Life* exclaimed in a 1954 article, "so much for so few." The article was accompanied by photographs of such novel phenomena as crowded student parking lots at a high school. It told of young men just out of college or the service who had their pick of excellent, high-paying jobs that would more than fulfill their parents' dreams for them.

"Never before" was virtually the slogan of the age. Never before had there been a car like this one or a floor wax like that one. The Populuxe generation heard of precedent being shattered several times each day.

Still, *Life* was onto something very important, and statistics bear it out. Americans who were born during the Depression came of age at a time when a number of economic and demographic factors converged in an extremely favorable way. There was more wealth to go around and a decline in the number of people to share it. Nothing like it had ever happened before, and nothing like it has happened since.

America had been able to turn its war machine into a consumer economy almost overnight. Productivity rose at a rate of better than 2 percent a year for most of the decade after World War II. American industry was using half the world's steel and oil. American consumers were able to buy three-quarters of

College was an important part of the middle-class experience—along with flying-saucer lamps and metal-framed furniture.

the cars and appliances on earth. Real income, after very modest inflation, was on the rise. Indeed, by 1953, the average income per person was half again the figure in 1929, and although the special conditions of the war made comparisons difficult, it is clear that nearly all this growth occurred after 1945.

A lot of this productivity gain came through the rebuilding of the nation's industrial plant into an increasingly automated system. An indication of this is that during these times of superheated economic growth, the number of people employed as laborers plummeted as a percentage of the work force, and even declined in absolute numbers. Yet this loss of jobs at the low end of the scale appeared, during the early 1950s at least, to cause no hardship whatsoever.

The reason was that better-paid jobs running or maintaining the machinery of automation increased much faster than the low-paid jobs were declining. People in factories, the very heart of the working class, were rapidly ascending to middle-class incomes. The average industrial wage rate had doubled from pre-Depression levels, and there were a lot more jobs available. And although such people typically had very high educational expectations for their children, they were able to achieve this higher status without a lot of preparation on their own part. They were in the right place at the right time.

The postwar period brought a much more equitable distribution of income than ever before. The increase in real income went almost entirely to the middle class. The absolute number of high-income people, which *Fortune* defined as those making more than $7,500 annually in 1953 dollars, more than doubled from 1929, but their share of the nation's total income declined sharply. The biggest increase came in the number of families in the $4,000–$7,000 salary range, which was understood to be solidly middle class. There were 5.5 million families in this category in 1929, 17.9 million in 1953. They accounted for 35 percent of the nation's population; they earned 42 percent of its income. These were the candidates for suburbia, the cream of the American market.

Unlike the classic definition of the middle class as a collection of small proprietors, this newly minted middle class was made up almost entirely of employees of corporations, and their income came almost entirely from salaries. Moreover, there was a decline in the number of families in the lowest income class, from 15.6 million to 11.7 million. The nation's total income was rising twice as rapidly as the population, so there was a lot more wealth per person. And the distribution of this new wealth was very fair, with average working people as the chief beneficiaries. By the beginning of the Populuxe era, America was materially more democratic than it had been at any time in its history.

Thus, when *Life* said so much was available for "so few," it was not speaking of a privileged elite. Rather it was pinpointing a striking demographic phenomenon. The decade of the Depression had produced the lowest American birthrate in the country's history and the smallest increase in absolute population since the decade of the Civil War. The first half of the 1940s, when so many men were at war, continued the slow population growth. The combination of an expanding economy and a declining employment pool made the transformation to an automated economy almost painless.

It also made the American dream of social and economic advancement much easier to realize. Colleges had spaces open for the sons and daughters of factory workers and truck drivers, and they were eager to have them. Their fathers might have to go into debt a bit to pay the tuition, but essentially they could afford to send their children to college. And upon graduation, there were plenty of managerial jobs, at least for the men. Many of the women became teachers and helped their families push higher into the middle class. Opportunity was abundant, and the obstacles to moving up the economic ladder were few. It is understandable that members of this generation felt that the sky was the limit.

But while the small birthrate during the 1930s made possible the painless industrial transformation and the optimism that characterized virtually the entire society, it also raised some potential problems. The American market was a wonder of the world, but what would happen when the number of consumers decreased?

Long lines at Levittown, Pennsylvania, for the unveiling of a new model in 1956. After 1954 even the basic Levitt house had become more elaborate.

The economic boom of the immediate postwar years represented an attempt by those who had lived through the Depression and World War II to catch up with their aspirations. People born during the teens and the twenties participated in the great buying spree, while those born during the thirties were not yet a factor in the market.

Those just starting households and having families constitute the group most desirable to home builders and manufacturers because they must make many large expenditures quickly. During the late 1940s and early 1950s, those doing so at a "normal" age were augmented by an enormous number of people who had delayed doing so because of the Depression and World War II. It was so large a market that industry had all it could do simply keeping up with it. From coast to coast, houses were selling as fast as they were built. Automobile ownership, a nearly universal dream, became a reality. The number of automobile registrations in the United States more than doubled during the decade after World War II.

The chief challenge for home builders, car manufacturers, furniture and appliance manufacturers and all the other segments of the consumer economy was to get the product out as quickly as possible and at an affordable price. Thus, although the immediate postwar homes have today been added to, elaborated and customized to the point that they are unrecognizable, they were, for the most part, sold as simple, bare-bones structures. They represented the desire to get a foot in the door, a step up the ladder.

Commentators like William H. Whyte deplored these "vast smog-filled deserts that are neither city, suburb nor country," but the purchasers of homes in the burgeoning subdivisions obviously saw things differently. Automobiles, too, stressed affordability and practicality. Furniture was never more straightforwardly a practical manufactured good than it was during the immediate postwar period. It was relatively easy to turn an economy that was organized for speedy war production to this great endeavor of deferred consumption. It worked. In absolute numbers, the amount of goods made available to the American people reached a peak not exceeded until the late 1960s.

It had long been obvious that this great spending spree could not continue indefinitely, and by 1952 businessmen began to worry. Not only were Americans finally catching up with their consumption, but the new prime generation of consumers that was about to come on line was the smallest ever. Either the end of the catch-up period or the decline in the population of the chief consuming generation could cause serious problems by themselves. Together, they portended disaster.

The population boom then under way was very apparent, and some firms, notably manufacturers of breakfast cereals, snacks and toys, began to turn children into a force in the economy. "Never underestimate the buying power of a child under seven," Dr. Frances Horwitch, Miss Frances of television's *Ding Dong School,* told a Chicago advertising conference in 1954. "He has brand loyalty and the determination to see that his parents purchase the product of his choice." Advertisers hardly needed the invitation of the kindly, ma-

The marionette Howdy Doody and his sidekick Buffalo Bob Smith were the stars of television's first hit children's program. Countless parents bought television sets so that the kids could watch Howdy Doody.

ternal psychologist to use television to induce children to whine, tug at their mothers' skirts and demand Rice Krispies, Sugar Pops, Ovaltine, Tom Corbett Space Cadet lunch boxes or Davy Crockett caps. Furniture makers geared up for playpens and cribs, and marketed fabrics and materials that were designed to stand up to spills and other forms of childish abuse. But the fact remained, as *Fortune* noted in 1953, that this group would not come into its own as consumers until 1965. Until then, business would have to find a way to continue to increase its revenue while facing a declining domestic market.

It was just at this moment during the early 1950s that the automobile industry faced a shakedown period. Studebaker merged with Packard, and Nash and Hudson became American Motors. Kaiser, the great wartime manufacturer, got out of the automobile business, except for making Jeeps. Kaiser's Henry J, which was variously described as looking like a deformed lemon and a metal egg, was a postwar prototype of the practical basic car, the four-wheeled equivalent of the Levitt house, a Volkswagen before its time. But it suffered from the fatal combination of appearing both too cheap and too weird. The Crosley also became a memory, and a dim one at that.

For the Big Three automakers, however, the solution emerged almost as soon as the problem came into focus. Automakers decided that if they were not going to sell more cars, they would have to sell more car.

The one good thing about this smaller generation was that it had more money to spend, and it wanted to spend it. With the addition of styling, decoration and fantasy to the car, the buyers would willingly part with more of their income. Besides, it didn't really hurt. As car prices went up, the percentage of income spent buying cars stayed about the same. The second part of the strategy, which was implicit in the first, was to encourage the frequent replacement of automobiles. By giving a car the same lifespan as a stylish dress, the Big Three could sell nearly as many cars as they had during periods when there were more potential buyers.

This yearly transformation of automobile models was terribly expensive, which was one reason why the smaller companies were not able to compete. But the unveiling of the new car models became a national ritual which inspired gossip beforehand and lavish color spreads in the magazines. And the companies also promoted their "cars of the future," which in retrospect looked like exaggerated versions of the quirkiest aspects of current models. At the time, however, they were marvelous demonstrations that the future was happening faster all the time, and the automakers were manufacturing the vehicles to get us there.

Nearly every industry followed the lead of the automobile companies, with more or less success. Home builders phased out the basic house and started coming up with new and elaborate models which could be fitted and personalized with a series of options and upgrades.

Furniture makers tried to follow this trend toward increasing fantasy and stylization, and certainly the artifacts that survive bear witness to the energy, creativity and sense of the outrageous that they brought to their task. The arrival of new materials, particularly new kinds of floor and wall coverings, brought distinctly new looks.

From both automobiles and clothing fashions came new colors and color combinations that rendered old rooms stodgy. The major decorating magazines initiated annual features on "this year's colors," which included complicated charts from which the reader could derive hundreds of stylish color schemes. "*House Beautiful* believes that one color alone is next to nothing," one version of this popular feature began. Many of the colors were like those you would see on the early color television sets that were just becoming available and in Technicolor movies—colors that did not seem to conform to anything seen in nature and were all the more wonderful because of that. Still, some years were far more turquoise than others. The increased importance of colors meant everything changed more often.

A new openness in house plans, in which the living and dining rooms often became mere incidents in a single large space, brought new kinds of furniture to compensate for the loss of walls. Chief among these was the storage unit that served as a room divider. In keeping with the ideal of openness, such furniture did not interrupt the flow of space, but it did demarcate areas into something rather like rooms.

Larger families and the arrival of the family room increased the demand for a new informal furniture that could stand up to children whose parents were loath to stifle their creativity and independence. A material like Naugahyde, an imitation leather which U.S. Rubber promoted heavily in the 1950s, answered all the demands of the time. It was very durable and safe from the ravages of all children who weren't carrying sharp instruments. Its nostalgic recollection of leather allowed the manufacturers of family-room furniture to democratize the great overstuffed chairs and sofas hitherto found mostly in gentlemen's clubs and private libraries. It was also manufactured in the most up-to-date colors.

Appliance manufacturers, some of which were owned by automobile companies, followed the same philosophy of bringing new looks and new features to familiar machines, while introducing many new products along the way. Appliances, which had taken on a streamlined form during preceding decades, became flatter and boxier, and they often sported decorative appliqués. They also were manufactured in color for the first time, something that introduced a new fashion element that was able to make kitchens and their appliances appear dated in a shorter time. But even though mid-1950s consumers had a real weakness for bright color contrasts, the two-toned refrigerator and stove never caught on.

The television set, a less practical and relatively new machine, went two-toned, modern, Early American, space age and every other trend that came along. Television, the most pervasive and influential novelty of the era, was widespread by 1954, and manufacturers were already starting to sell people on the idea of a second set for the kids, or for the bedroom, and also to gear up for the arrival of color. Not even the magic box could escape the implications of the demographic trough.

The new world without sidewalks was, at once, an exciting and perplexing place. It was a world of the young, a place apart from mothers and uncles and familiar neighbors. You were new, and so were all your neighbors. And in many suburbs the chances were that neither you nor they would be in the neighborhood very long. Nationwide, one American in five moved every year, but in

With the moving van idling in the background, the first family to move into Levittown, New Jersey, waits as William J. Levitt cuts the ribbon. The fellow with the pipe is the mayor of the township, which would never be the same.

fast-changing areas like the San Fernando Valley in Los Angeles or Nassau County on Long Island, more than 40 percent of the houses changed hands each year. Working-class families, even in the suburbs, moved far less often than the average, but young families in which the husband was making his way up the corporate ladder moved frequently. Corporate America was increasingly dispersed, and organizations were larger and farther-flung than ever. The transfer was a way of life. It was usually welcome because moving elsewhere almost always meant moving up, or it at least carried that promise.

The mobility of these trend-setting suburbanites probably contributed to the increasing uniformity of suburbs from coast to coast as new styles, products and trends hit the housing market. Such standardization had its value for the highly mobile segment of the suburban population. If your company moved you from Cherry Hill, New Jersey, to Anaheim, California, the vegetation would be different, but you could probably move into much the same house. Your furniture would fit, and it would be blessedly familiar besides.

This might be what caused problems for the furniture industry, which never performed as well during this period as other manufacturers of household products. Furniture could be moved, and it provided that quality of permanence and familiarity that mitigated the disorientation and pain of corporate nomadism. At the same time, the new house and the new neighborhood satisfied the craving for a change of scenery that might lead a more settled person to throw out the furniture and start over. Major appliances are heavy, bulky and cold; they elicit fewer emotional attachments and are more likely to be discarded and left behind. Besides, the fully equipped modern kitchen with built-in appliances was an important selling point in housing developments, and buyers were more than happy to have the cost of the appliances absorbed into their mortgages.

How do you get people to buy appliances and furniture when their old ones aren't broken? Sell stylish new colors, of course. Two-toned refrigerators never really made it, however.

This itinerant young suburban market was far from a majority of the American people, but it was considered the cream of the market and it set the tone for the rest. The look and accessories of casual suburban living moved quickly into older urban row-house neighborhoods, and suburbanites set the goals to strive for. In some part of his being, every American wanted a Cadillac. And even though television and magazines united the country as never before, the amount of contact Americans had with other people was steadily diminishing as they drove to where they were going and stayed away from the crowds and jostling of the cities.

The mass market was not the masses of the cities. It was an aggregation of individuals and families, living apart, addressed through the mass media. Indeed, in retrospect, many of the chief causes of the civil rights movement seem anachronistic, because they sought inclusion in the public life of America at the same time that the mass public was retreating from such activities as riding buses and sending children to urban schools.

It was an article of faith that the style of America was being set in the suburbs. What was true and measurable was that people in suburbs were buying more than their share of what America was producing, and that any manufacturer who did not take special pains to meet this market was probably going to be in trouble. In 1953, suburbanites accounted for about 20 percent of the population, but more than 30 percent of those of middle income or higher were in the suburbs. Even though this was a period of increasing fairness in income distribution, the suburbs were beginning to get richer and richer, while the residents of cities got poorer and poorer.

During the first years of the 1950s, the prototypical average American— the kind that is shown in magazine and television advertisements, situation-comedy programs, elementary school textbooks and almost all media that were intended to have mass appeal—moved out of the cities. The first generation of television programs, such as *The Life of Riley, The Honeymooners* and *I Love Lucy,* had urban settings. When Lucy and Ricky moved from their Manhattan apartment house to Westport, Connecticut, and took their erstwhile landlord and landlady, Fred and Ethel Mertz, with them, it showed that even the most successful institution had to make the move to suburbia to maintain credibility with the audience. Besides, Little Ricky was getting big, and you couldn't bring him up properly in the city. They spoke of Westport, which was even then a very suburban place, as "the country," and even more of the television programs were set in specifically rural or small-town settings. Political scientists and sociologists found that people who were moving to the suburbs liked to think they were moving to small towns.

The new suburbanites were attractive consumers, and almost everything they encountered in the popular media treated them as consumers. Moreover, because they were usually far from their families and others who would traditionally set standards for them, they were considered to be a very malleable market. They were very receptive to newness, they believed that things were improving. They watched a lot of television and read a lot of magazines, from which they were believed to be taking ideas about how they should live. In short, they were ideal targets for advertising.

One indication that this was true could be seen in the way people ate. In the early 1950s, a very unusual thing happened. Americans increased the percentage of their income they were willing to spend on food. No industry marketed more aggressively or came up with a larger array of new, more profitable products. Food was more than mere nourishment; it was convenience, modernity and a fulfillment of parental obligations. A bit of the increased expenditure came from moving up in status—eating high on the hog—but most came in manufactured food, such as canned goods, frozen foods, boxed mixes, prepared snacks. A few ounces of flour could be sold for much more as part of a prepared cake mix, and a chicken leg carried a far higher price tag, and profit margin, as a component of a TV dinner than it did in the butcher's case. These varied, easy-to-prepare foods were all lined up on the counters of that new institution, the supermarket, whose long aisles and overflowing shelves exposed more products than was possible in the ordinary grocery store and whose generous parking lots made it easier for buyers to carry it all home.

"Never has so much been available to so many as now," wrote food writer Poppy Cannon in a typical fit of 1953 euphoria. "And the can opener!" she apostrophized a bit later in the article. "That *open sesame* to wealth and freedom . . . Freedom from tedium, space, work, and your own inexperience."

Poppy Cannon's four freedoms were a far cry from FDR's, but they spoke to real concerns of her readers. The last one, inexperience, was particularly crucial, since Mother wasn't around to give guidance. It was reassuring to have a respected food writer endorse convenience and celebrate the opening of a can, even as part of a meal you make for company.

Recipes found on the backs of cans and boxes became increasingly influential during this period. Typically there were directions for the preparation of the product and suggestions about how to use the product to make a fancier "company" dish. Just as basic automobiles were made more exciting by the addition of tailfins and chrome, so were ordinary sweet potatoes dressed up by the addition of Campfire marshmallows and Dole crushed pineapple. Just as buyers of automobiles and other products knew that styling was a bit fraudulent, eaters seemed to enjoy the revelation that the apple pie was really made out of Ritz crackers and the snack at the party was just plain old Wheat Chex putting on airs.

The recipe that truly sums up Populuxe living first appeared in 1954 on the back of the box of Lipton's dehydrated onion soup mix. It was called California dip, and it was concocted simply by mixing the powder inside the box with processed sour cream, itself a relatively unfamiliar product that through this recipe escaped its ethnic associations and went mainstream. Using potato chips as little shovels, you gathered up the deliciously salty but drip-prone liquid and popped it, potato chip and all, into your mouth as quickly and gracefully as possible. There was anxiety in all this—particularly the fear that a

Americans increased the percentage of their income they spent on food during the Populuxe years, a phenomenon that was helped along by a new way of shopping, the supermarket. These immense, modern stores displayed more kinds of products in one place than had ever been seen before. When new ones opened, they often drew crowds.

Food accounted for an increasing share of larger household budgets. It was sold along with a lot of advice from figures like Betty Crocker, or in new, convenient forms, such as the TV dinner.

great glop of the stuff would land on your tie or the rug—but also immense satisfaction. With chip and dip, the technology of junk food reached a culinary and artistic pinnacle.

It is probable that few chip-and-dip eaters considered the snack as a purely visual phenomenon, but with decades of perspective it is easy to see how perfectly it fit into their environment. Formally, the potato chip, with its free-form shape and doubly curving plane, recalled some of the high-design objects of the day, Danish coffee tables and American molded fiberglass and bent plywood chairs. Formally, it is a very short jump from the standard potato chip to the great double-curving furniture of Charles Eames and Eero Saarinen.

And to this manufactured object was added that extra something that was understood to transform it. Serving plain potato chips to guests was not quite enough. But with the addition of dip, the stopgap snack turned into a party. Visually, the simple, graceful potato chip looks as overloaded as, for example, the 1959 Cadillac, whose lethally-sharp-looking tailfins had sprouted rocket-shaped taillights that seemed to be clinging precariously to their sides. The dip ruined the pure form of the chip, but it added symbolic weight. It also added physical weight that often cracked the chip. The engineering solution was the corrugated chip, whose form presaged the ridged concrete roof found on so much roadside architecture around the turn of the 1960s.

This new kind of food also generated its own container, the chip and dip set in which a large bowl for the chips, often a free-form shape, had cantilevered from it a small bowl that held the dip. This cantilever echoed the structural nature of chip and dip itself.

The negligible preparation time of chip and dip was also significant, since it made spur-of-the moment entertaining much easier. One premise of suburban living was informality and spontaneity. With chip and dip, one could entertain at a moment's notice. And even though studies later indicated that suburbanites weren't much more informal and spontaneous than anyone else, it was not much trouble to keep the ingredients around, just in case someone came by. And it was delicious.

Chip and dip was a thoroughly modern food, not something your mother would have told you about. Even as Americans became more and more widely dispersed geographically, they became more and more a single nation, all making the same recipes found on the backs of boxes. Betty Crocker represented a new kind of authority, acting *in loco parentis*.

Authorities and experts seemed everywhere in the popular media, in editorial copy, advertising and often both. They served as national parents, telling young people separated from their families and thrown into unfamiliar contexts how to deal with their problems, raise their children, take care of their house and yard, dress, entertain and enjoy themselves.

Folk wisdom, the sort of thing your family might tell you, was called into serious question by the rapidly changing circumstances of modern life. Parents wondering about what to do about their children were more likely to consult— and believe—Dr. Spock's child-rearing manual than their own parents, who had been through it all before. One major reason was the new belief in psychology, which was popularized in newspapers and magazines and made its way into teacher training and management. It represented a whole new kind

Lipton's "Festive California Dip," shown here with corrugated potato chips, whose extra strength allowed for heavy-duty dipping.

of authority, one which seemed to counsel ignoring everything your parents might tell you.

Advertisers used the new interest in popular psychology to give additional weight to unsurprising assertions. "It's a psychological fact: *Pleasure helps your disposition,*" declared a 1955 advertisement for Camel cigarettes. Then, after claiming scientific authority for the benefit of smoking, the advertisement used another form of respected authority of the time, a retired general, to assert that Camels offer more pure pleasure than just about anything else. The psychology was there to appeal to women, while the general's endorsement spoke to men. Neither was exactly an appeal to reason.

Today, the fantasies and aspirations that were being sold along with products during the Populuxe era seem so apparent as to be almost laughable. But at the time, people were a bit more naïve and a bit more receptive to the skills of advertising, marketing and packaging. Vance Packard's best-selling book on the psychological dimensions of advertising, *The Hidden Persuaders,* came as a shock to many consumers when it appeared in 1957, although the methods discussed seem fairly blatant today. The book was strident in its condemnation of the way in which advertising experts manipulate consumers, and it almost certainly overstated the power of advertising to change people's behavior. At the same time, it couldn't help but evoke admiration for the cleverness of the industry, how much it had learned about people and the wit with which it used the information. People enjoy being fooled creatively, never more so than during the Populuxe era. Was convincing people that a detergent is mild by putting it in a blue box and that it is powerful by using an orange box any more fraudulent than a car that copies the look of an airplane or an apple pie made out of crackers? All were more often admired than condemned.

Anyone who paid attention to all the experts and all the advertising, and tried to behave accordingly, would probably have gone mad from trying to reconcile the many contradictions routinely set forth in the popular magazines.

Men were to be consummate breadwinners, protectors of their family, who journeyed to work each day to do their part for the most productive and robust economy the world had ever seen. They were told that they must be close to their families and to their houses. *Life* discovered in suburbia "the new domesticated male" and noted that he typically had three children at the age his father was when he married. Men were believed to be taking an ever larger share in the tasks of keeping a household together, and these chores seemed to become more important as home and family were increasingly depicted as the only respectable obsessions. Lawns had to be attended to. Men were emissaries of modern styles from their workplaces to their homes, and they should assist their wives in deciding how to decorate those homes. And the man was expected to be a do-it-yourselfer, getting special rewards from solving the crises of the homeowner while steadily improving his investment. He was the support on which the household rested, and the stability of his family's life was a very important goal. Yet he was also married to his employer and expected to uproot his family and take it off to distant places to serve the company. He was,

IT'S A PSYCHOLOGICAL FACT: **PLEASURE HELPS YOUR DISPOSITION**

How's your disposition today?

EVER FEEL LIKE SQUAWKING? That's only human when little annoyances peck at you. But remember this psychological fact: pleasure helps your disposition. Everyday pleasures, like smoking for instance, are important. So if you're a smoker, you're wise to choose the cigarette that gives the *most* pleasure. And that's Camel!

For **more** pure pleasure_have a **Camel**

"They've got what it takes!"
Claire L. Chennault
Major General (Ret.) USAF

R. J. Reynolds Tobacco Company, Winston-Salem, N. C.

GENERAL CHENNAULT says: "Camels have traveled with me for over 40 years. To me, no other cigarette tastes so good yet smokes so smooth and mild as Camel!" General Chennault agrees with millions of smokers — there's *more pure pleasure* in Camels. And pleasure, remember, helps your disposition. So have a Camel — America's first-choice cigarette!

No other cigarette is so rich-tasting, yet so mild!

at once, more domesticated and more career-oriented than his father, and he did not have the support of old friends and nearby family to help him through difficult times.

He was likely to be the first member of his family to be doing well economically, and he was part of a generation of pioneers in the new kind of suburbia that was emerging. Still, he was constantly being reassured that his kind of life was normal. He was not defeated by these contradictions. He consistently told pollsters that he was happy, that his chief regret was that he did not have more education, that he expected to do better next year and that his children would do even better than he did.

"It's twice as simple to be an easygoing host when you're unhampered by confined areas and indoor formality." That's what the original caption said. It didn't mention all the special equipment needed to roast a duck in the yard.

While women were rarely assumed to have a productive place in the economy, they were taken very seriously as consumers and indeed were often depicted as the chief decision makers in regard to what their families would purchase. They were marrying younger than their mothers had, and their husbands were younger too. That made more children, indeed a lot of children all at once, nearly inevitable.

The physical nature of most suburbs, with their lack of public facilities and public transportation, increased the demands on mothers, even those of older, theoreticaly more self-sufficient children. They organized their children's social life and their educational and athletic achievement. One of the most prevalent commercial images of Mom was behind the wheel of a station wagon, sitting at a curbside while pigtailed Susie and freckled-faced Tommy come running to be picked up from ballet lessons or Little League. (On Saturday, Dad took the station wagon, usually down to the lumberyard to buy plywood.)

Around the house, Mom was said to be an engineer, someone who keeps a technologically and organizationally complex institution running smoothly. In advertising at least, she did not have to exert herself very much. If anyone was depicted on her hands and knees scrubbing a floor it was someone from her parents' generation, before the availability of modern cleansers and labor-saving appliances. Women in magazines were always stylishly and impractically dressed. In advertising, they sometimes wore a glove to press the button of the latest household machine. More often than you would expect, they were shown striking poses in the kitchen while wearing a tiara. Somebody must have liked this, because the image persisted for many years.

This fit in with the woman's other cherished role, as "glamour girl" for her weary husband, as well as counselor and confidante. "The two big steps that women must take are to help their husbands decide where they are going and

Dad might use some of his extra time to coach a Little League team. This woman is doing her laundry. But because her washer is equipped with a three-ring agitator, she feels like a queen.

use their pretty heads to help get them there," wrote Mrs. Dale Carnegie in the April 1955 *Better Homes and Gardens*. "Let's face it, girls. That wonderful guy in your house—and in mine—is building your house, your happiness and the opportunities that will come to your children." And she warned: "Split levels may be fine and exciting when you're planning your house. But there is simply no room for split level thinking—or doing—when Mr. and Mrs. set their sights on a happy home, a host of friends and a bright future through success in HIS job." So there.

The polls generally found women slightly less happy than their husbands, although far more satisfied than not. They expressed extreme displeasure with housework, perhaps because the media were leading them to believe that they would not have to do any. They said they wanted more excitement in their lives. And by 1959 teenage girls were saying that they planned to have a career outside of the home.

It was difficult to live up to the image of the new suburban man and woman found in mass magazines, television and advertising. On top of this was tremendous criticism that emanated from intellectuals and was often disseminated through these very same outlets. Chief among these critiques were

that suburbanites were abject conformists without any minds of their own. They were dupes whose culture had been sugar-coated by hucksters, and they chose to live in what Lewis Mumford called "the proliferating nonentity" of suburbia. Their environment was not paradise, as everyone knew, nor was it countryside or the relatively more privileged suburbs known to previous generations, something that commentators spent quite a lot of time deploring.

There was a distinct class bias in most of what was written about suburbia and suburbanites during this time. For most intellectuals, it represented not a triumph of democracy but a proof of Robert Maynard Hutchins' formulation that the industrial revolution made it possible for a moron to be successful. There arose a successful minor genre of trouble-in-the-suburbs literature, with such titles as *The Crack in the Picture Window,* the story of John and Mary Drone and the way in which development living drives them crazy, without their knowing it. One of the most extreme was *The Split Level Trap,* based on the experiences of a psychiatrist in a northern New Jersey suburb. Things were so bad out there, he wrote, that the phenomenon should be renamed. He proposed Disturbia.

Suburbia was, above all, grassy. Lawns require attention, but this was viewed as recreation, not work.

One of the problems that commentators seemed to have had was that they had far higher expectations for suburbia than the residents themselves had. Suburbia was where new houses were, where there were yards and barbecues. Buyers of development houses knew they were not getting a carefully landscaped, picturesque environment. The neighbors of sociologist Herbert Gans, who in 1958 was one of the first people to move into the third Levittown, now Willingboro, New Jersey, told him they hardly thought about a new community or a new environment when they were making their decisions. They were there because Levittown offered the most house for the money. In a few cases where chunks of whole urban neighborhoods moved en masse to a particular suburb or when an industrial plant relocated, people were able to simply transplant the society with which they were comfortable. Many people changed the way they lived upon moving to suburbia, but that was a by-product, not a goal.

Some of the anti-suburban commentary of the period seems fired by anger at many new suburbanites betraying their working-class backgrounds by voting for Eisenhower. Later it became clear that they had not all metamorphosed into Republicans, but rather that they voted for someone who represented the same kind of security and stability they looked for in their neighborhoods and within their families.

Even the reputation for conformity has probably been overstated. One of the hallmarks of suburbia was, in fact, a lack of the standards and expectations one would find in an ethnic neighborhood of a large city or in a small town. The suburbs were inhabited by people who didn't know one another, let alone their neighbors' parents, who had never lived in such a place before and weren't quite sure of how to do it. And like most people in such a novel situation, they suspected that other people really knew how to behave. They might criticize how their neighbors were bringing up their children, but they looked to their neighbors for signals on how to behave.

In the 1950s and early 1960s, most suburban places had not been around long enough to have become communities, a situation that was exacerbated by the extreme mobility of their residents. They felt anxiety about how to fit into a society whose shape and rules were more or less indeterminate. Far from being conformist, many suburbs were highly tolerant, more tolerant than the communities from which most of their residents had moved. In both city and small town, worry over what the neighbors would think kept people in line. In the suburbs, one had little idea of what the neighbors were doing inside their houses and was reluctant to disapprove.

Yet there were new situations to confront, new etiquette to be formulated in order to keep things humming in at least apparent harmony. Sometimes the atmosphere of mutual unfamiliarity led to the kind of social horror story Gans came across in Levittown, New Jersey. A couple newly arrived from New York invited some neighbors for a cocktail party. The hostess wore Capri pants for the occasion. Early arrivals, who saw the hostess through the window, noticed her unfamiliar outfit and concluded that she was in her pajamas. Had they shown up on the wrong night? What sort of a woman wears her pajamas in front of company? They went back home and telephoned other neighbors who were going to the party and spread doubt throughout the neighborhood. Despite grave doubts and much social discomfort, the party finally took place. Eventually, the hostess heard about what happened and the Capri pants were put in the closet and left there. Such incidents were common and disconcerting. New people and new situations bring new hazards.

It was important to show respect for the community that wasn't quite there, which was one reason why lawns were so important. The ideal of continuous rolling lawns was widely shared and hardly ever questioned. Transgressors—people who did not care for their lawns zealously enough or mow frequently enough—were subject to considerable social pressure. There were enough such people to eventually lead many suburban communities to enact nuisance laws that required that lawns be kept almost as short as men's hair.

The maintenance of the suburban landscape evoked a mixture of cooperation and competition from homeowners. Nearly everyone shared the vision of continuous, unobstructed, well-manicured lawns, which each homeowner had a duty to maintain. It was a great time to be in the grass seed business, and as

U.S. News & World Report concluded at the end of a 1956 special report on the suburbs, the outlook for plants, shrubs, lawn mowers, garden tractors and household tools was rosy for at least another decade.

At the same time, residents felt a pride of ownership, a need to demarcate their particular pieces of the earth. Showing up your neighbor by having a greener and more weed-free lawn was a subtle way of claiming the land, but fences are more visible to the average passerby. However, fences work against the image of continuous lawn. The solution was the symbolic fences—a few lengths of split rail or a bit of picket fence in the front yard—that established boundaries without disturbing the pastoral continuity. For years, *House Beautiful* campaigned for high, effective fences, often taking a political tack: "The fence creates a small private world for you and yours. Today, that is exactly what communists and bureaucrats and authoritarians want to destroy." Nevertheless, such fences were generally disapproved of even more strongly than unmowed lawns. Because you only erected such a barrier out of utter loathing for your neighbors, these became known as "spite fences," and they were almost universally illegal.

A high fence or a weedy lawn was an affront to the neighbors and, because such phenomena were visible signs of disharmony, a possible threat to property values. People who expected to move regularly looked for houses in areas that appreciated in value and would be easy to sell when the time came. Neighbors might disagree on everything else, but on the need to maintain property values, it was easy to come together.

For all the apparent openness of suburbia—the picture windows through which it was possible to view your neighbor's furniture and family activities, the lack of effective fences between properties—there were few institutions that could truly foster the building of a community.

At the time, commentators on suburbia criticized their residents for what they found to be an almost hysterical involvement in community organizations. Sociologists who did case studies found that things were not quite as frantic as they appeared, but that there was a proliferation of new organizations. Most of these were attempts to find other people like oneself. One of the most pronounced phenomena was the flurry of Jews founding synagogues, even though many of those doing so had not attended services in the past. In general, the synagogues existed for children's classes and for ancillary social organizations rather than for the practice of the faith, something that worried Jewish leaders. Similar things were happening in many of the Protestant denominations, although in some cases the move to suburbia was the opportunity to go shopping for a new denomination that offered more social prestige or a more appealing preacher.

The concerns that affected just about everybody in a suburban community were schools and taxes, but these often proved to be issues that provoked division rather than cohesion within the community. One matter on which suburbanites tended to agree was that they should keep their government small and local, rather than to join in regional government or merge with cities, as

Tupperware parties did not merely sell plastic containers. They also provided an opportunity for arm's-length sociability.

most experts were proposing at the time. Their little old governments were a recollection of small-town living, something American folklore tends to idealize.

The one thing nearly all suburbanites had in common was that they were consumers. Buying things provided that common ground for that characteristic and peculiar social institution, the Tupperware party. God may or may not have been the most important element in suburban religion, but it is clear that Tupperware was not the most important aspect of a Tupperware party.

Tupperware, a line of tight-topped plastic refrigerator storage containers, was developed by Earl Tupper immediately after World War II. The objects were simple, straightforward and, for their time, technologically innovative. And unlike most manufacturers, who faced the marketing challenges of the mid-1950s by decorating the products, giving them stars and boomerangs and making them tilt, Tupper kept his line simple. Tupperware became increasingly useful, of course, as the sales of frost-free refrigerators increased and threatened chilled food with dehydration. But the chief weapon, and most brilliant marketing ploy, was the home party where a hostess would invite people over for a demonstration of the products. The hostess would get gifts from Tupperware, depending on the volume sold at her party. And nobody would leave without at least one piece of Tupperware. Tupper did not invent the home party—it was a prewar innovation—but his firm did perfect it.

At the time, some cynics labeled such parties commercial transactions masquerading as social events. This was true, from the company's point of view. But for those who gave the parties and those who attended them, it was more like a party disguised as a commercial transaction. The fact of the Tupperware made invitations easier to issue to those you might not know very well.

If they didn't want to come, they could always say they didn't need any Tupperware. For someone who was invited but wasn't sure whether she liked the hostess, it was a low-risk situation. Usually, one wasn't expected to reciprocate an invitation to a Tupperware party, so if it all turned out to be a mistake, you could get out of it by buying a translucent butter dish. If the hostess didn't like the people she invited, at least she'd get Tupperware, and possibly even an electric frying pan. In short, the presence of the Tupperware freed the party from most of its uncertainty.

And on the more positive side, it provided a common activity, one that did not have to be particularly personal or intimate. Despite the cult of informality in the suburbs, such opportunities seem to have been rare and welcome. Suburbia was a strange, new, insecure place. In most Populuxe products, symbolic decoration was added to mass-produced objects in order to invoke the past and the future and help the new suburbanites express the new kind of lives they were living. Rather than adding decoration to its products, Tupperware added a ritual, the party, which helped new suburbanites deal with the insecurity and loneliness that was part of their pioneering lives. The company added the ritual for the same reason that most manufacturers added the decorations. It sold the product effectively, using an emotional approach. Suburbanites were understood primarily as America's top consumers, and they were urged to express themselves by buying, and then buying some more.

A New Place

Today, suburbia is the normal habitat of Americans, such a pervasive element in our culture that it requires an act of imagination to cast your mind back only a few decades to the time when a nation's way of life, and its landscape, was reinvented. People were able to buy homes more easily than ever before, and the home became the focus for a way of living, and a way of consuming, the likes of which the world had never seen. The generation that created suburbia as we know it was made up of the best consumers, and they made America go. Their tastes and their habits were shaped by advertising, then tested by consumer polling. The ability to have so great a choice of things to buy was viewed as a fulfillment of the promise of democracy. Never had so many people had so broad a choice of things they could acquire, and never had the gap between that which was available only to the rich and that attainable by the masses appeared to be so small.

In the newly invented world of the mass suburbs, possessions clearly played an extremely important role. But who were these status seekers trying to impress? "Their neighbors" is the obvious answer, and there was, no doubt, an aspect of "keeping up with the Joneses." But that phrase, though it was one of the clichés of the time, makes the endeavor appear more competitive than it really was. Your family and the Joneses were not struggling to outdo one another. Some sociological studies done at the time suggest that the opposite took place: neighbors informally set standards and indirectly punished those who made purchases that were needlessly luxurious and ostentatious. Rather than being weapons in a war of status, the objects were marks of belonging. The Joneses and everyone else were newcomers to a way of life that had not existed before World War II. You wanted to have possessions that were at least as good as your neighbors', but there was no point in standing far out of the mainstream. The alternative was to move to a more congenial neighborhood.

The consensus of where the mainstream was developed very quickly, as appliance manufacturers discovered during the early 1950s when they brought out a parade of new products they hoped would be mainstays of the new suburban households. Some, like the automatic clothes washer, and later the dryer, took hold right away. Some, such as the freestanding deep freeze, had a flurry of sales when they were first introduced. But after the early buyers suffered frostbite while trying to pry indeterminate chunks of food from glacial formations deep in these cold coffins, they virtually disappeared from the market. The deep freeze had not been accepted as a standard item for modern living. Later, of course, it re-emerged as an ever-larger compartment of the steadily expanding refrigerator. Likewise, dishwasher sales fell flat soon after the product was introduced. Finally, nearly a decade later, manufacturers mounted a successful campaign to induce developers to build them into the kitchens of their new houses. Only then did a substantial number of individuals go out and buy dishwashers.

Everything a family owned—the house, the car, the furniture—was provisional. Even if it didn't wear out, there was always the hope of being able to move up the ladder and buy something better. "People buy houses the way they used to buy cars," a suburban Los Angeles real estate salesman said in a 1957 *Newsweek* special report on the suburbs. He didn't add that automobile manufacturers were selling cars with an approach similar to that typically associated with clothes and that the idea of buying a new car every year no longer seemed to be an outrageous extravagance. It was not universal or typical, but it was a goal many people were striving for. Moreover, technology was making strides, and it seemed reasonable to assume that the products available were actually improving. And precisely because people did not expect to hold on to possessions for the rest, or even for very much, of their lives, it became all right for these to become fun, fashionable and fantastic.

To these might be added a fourth F, futuristic. This was a time that truly believed in the future. The imagery of the jet plane, which merged with that of the rocket and the conquest of space, had a strong hold on the public imagination. These had their dark side, of course, and fear of the Soviet Union and fear of nuclear warfare showed up strongly in most surveys of American attitudes during this period. Still, in a 1959 Gallup poll on Americans' views of the future, even a majority of those who believed that nuclear war was likely also believed that life would continue to improve year by year.

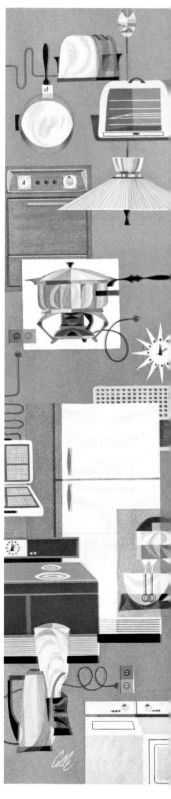

Such anxiety over public events, such as war or economic depression, were minor compared with more personal anxieties, such as whether the family would be able to make ends meet or whether there would be enough money to send the children to college. In advertisements, anxieties about home and family occasionally took on bizarre forms. One series of insurance ads depicted the typical suburban dream house, with shutters and a large front lawn. Things are going wrong, however. Someone is falling into a hole in the front lawn, someone else is falling off a ladder, and in a touch of danger that made the whole tableau thoroughly up-to-date, an airplane had crashed into the roof. Thus did the most pervasive symbol of modernity hit home.

While the airplane and the rocket may have been the most important symbols of the future, the most concrete affirmation of faith in the future was the birth of babies in record numbers. Lurking in their playpens, or romping from yard to yard, were the baby-boomers, the children who were so often cited as the reason for it all. Populuxe was the environment of their childhood, which perhaps explains why so many of them want to recover some of the mementos of that time. Indeed, some social critics of the era referred to American society of the time as "a filiarchy," ruled by children, whose perceived needs, and cries of "I want my Maypo," drove the entire economy. Between 1947 and 1961, births alone accounted for population increases of significantly more than 2 percent and sometimes as much as 2.5 percent a year. Nearly every poll done during the period indicated that parents placed children and family life as not only their highest priority but also their greatest satisfaction. The children may not have been ruling from their high-chair thrones, but their parents were convinced that their own role in life was to make a world for their children that was better than the unstable decades of war and privation in which they had grown up. They did it "for the kids."

Suburbia was justified primarily as the ideal environment in which to bring up children. Basically this was because they could go out and play in the yard with safety, and even the circle and cul-de-sac street pattern slowed cars down sufficiently to cut down on danger. Critics of suburbia argued that it wasn't a good place for children at all. They pointed out that there were fewer parks, playing fields and playgrounds than in typical urban neighborhoods. Suburban children had fewer opportunities to be independent and relied on their mothers to enable them to play and socialize with school friends and others. Most of these criticisms were valid, and as children grew older, most suburban communities made investments in playgrounds, pools, skating rinks and other facilities to accommodate them. But the major question of whether suburbia was the best place for children was rarely addressed because it seemed self-evident that it was.

Children might have been the excuse but they were not the reason for the massive move to suburbia during the years after World War II. Suburbanization had long been equated with moves up the economic and status ladder in America, and the cities were viewed with suspicion from the very founding of the country. Probably the earliest American suburbs were planned by William

Juggling your protection can cost you plenty!

Modern living brought all sorts of new conveniences—and headaches, too.

A post–World War II suburban vista: small houses, curving streets, tricycles, and very young trees.

Penn when in 1682 he allocated a strip of countryside just beyond the limits of Philadelphia for non-farming country houses. He called them Liberty Lands. Walt Disney himself could scarcely have done better. During the mid-nineteenth century the suburban villa, as depicted in popular magazines and in architectural pattern books, became the first popular American dream house. It was most often shown in a pastoral setting, neither strictly agrarian nor wilderness. The house was typically picturesque in its general aspect, asymmetrical in its composition, and exhibited some interpretation of Gothic or Italianate in its architectural style.

When such buildings were actually erected, however, they were not in some remote glade but fairly close together in neighborhoods that are today considered to be unambiguously urban. These were the suburbs made possible by the horse-drawn, and later the electrified, streetcar. Their principal significance was that they were remote from factories and shops where money was made. Because public transportation was a luxury during most of the nineteenth century, only the well-to-do could afford such suburban living.

Commuter railroads, running on their own rights-of-way, made possible even greater dispersion of the population. Los Angeles, for example, took on its many-centered, not too dense configuration largely because of its famous interurban system, the Big Red Cars. Some of these suburbs, such as Cleveland's Shaker Heights and Philadelphia's Chestnut Hill, were developed by entrepreneurs who had a social goal—to mold from the children of industrialists a true American aristocracy. The buildings were designed to appear old upon completion, to create the illusion they had always been there. Their architecture resembled that of the Ivy League and other prestigious colleges, and for much the same reason. Suburban living was seen as gracious and elite.

During the years between World War I and World War II, some suburban areas began to be more than bedrooms. The Country Club district of Kansas City offered a complete alternative to downtown, with many shops arranged in a delightful, eclectic Spanish-style environment. There was even a hotel. In Los Angeles, Bullocks Wilshire invented the form of the department store with parking lot. The typical American department store had stood at the center of cities' transportation systems, but by the 1930s there was money to be made away from downtown from people in cars.

The Depression brought the beginning of the infrastructure that made the postwar sprawl possible, with the building of parkways around New York City and the first freeways in Los Angeles. The network of parkways Robert Moses built around New York was supposed to facilitate recreational driving. Its effect was to make the automobile an important supplement to the commuter rail system, if not its replacement. The General Motors Futurama at the 1939 New York World's Fair provided a vision of automobiles speeding down multilane limited-access highways that made Moses' parkways look like cow paths. People emerged from that popular exhibit wearing buttons that said "I have seen the future." That vision received so much attention and was so widely known that the shape the nation would take in the post-Depression era seemed foreordained. America was ready to move out.

Thus, the mass exodus to suburbia was not really a revolutionary idea. Indeed, people were fully expecting it to happen. Even during World War II, there were books and articles about "your new postwar home." Such writings made three important assumptions. The first was that there would be a new postwar home for a significant portion of the population. The second assumption was that it would be built new for modern living, that it would not be an older house adapted for contemporary needs. Indeed, except for the occasional

Sometimes, realization fell short of the developer's promise. And the early years of a suburb always had a lot of dust and mud.

restored eighteenth-century Connecticut farmhouse or hundred-year-old barn with modern insides, older houses virtually disappeared from home and decorating magazines until well into the 1960s. And the third assumption was that it would be suburban. The cities were full, the writers said. They were not really suitable. In fact, they were hardly considered.

Besides, there was some truth to the belief that the cities were full. Unlike the urban slums of today, in which many houses are simply abandoned and population density is low, postwar cities had large districts where it was not uncommon for several families to be crowded into tiny houses and apartments. Clearing the slums and spreading out the population was an important part of the liberal agenda during the immediate postwar era, although nobody could have predicted how rapidly this would take place and what negative consequences it would have for the cities.

The doubling of homeownership that occurred during the postwar era was made possible by the transformation of the home-building industry. Although it never became the General Motors-like industry many predicted, home building benefited from sophisticated management and economies of scale. The time it took to build a house was reduced to no more than six weeks, less than half the prewar time. But in order to be affordable for buyers and profitable for builders, such houses had to be repetitive in their construction and built on flat, inexpensive land. Because agriculture was becoming increasingly efficient and centralized, farmers at the edges of urban areas were often eager to sell. The housing boom could have happened nowhere else.

But it is unlikely that it could ever have happened at all without the intervention of the federal government through Federal Housing Administration mortgage insurance and Veterans Administration mortgage guarantees. The VA made it possible for boys who had gone off to war from these overcrowded city streets to jump several steps up the social ladder and buy a house in the suburbs. "No down payment for Veterans!" was the promise of nearly every real estate developer during the mid-1950s. The GI Bill put a lot of developers, not all of them honest, into business. There were countless stories of developers walking away and leaving streets unpaved, lots without landscaping and neighborhoods without sewers. Still, it really was cheaper for a veteran to buy than to rent, and he didn't need capital. As California developer Ned Eichler has recalled, disgruntled home buyers would often complain that they had put every dime they had into the house. "'Every dime' in such cases was often as little as $100 or $200 for closing costs," Eichler wrote.

In each of the years between 1947 and 1957, the percentage of houses sold with VA or FHA mortgages ranged from just under 40 percent to more than 50 percent, more than enough for these programs to have determined the shape of the entire new-housing market during this period. And both agencies concentrated their investment on new buildings in the suburbs, while ignoring the cities.

One important justification for such policies stemmed from the experience of World War II in which sustained aerial bombing of urban areas played such a major role. The loss of most of the Pacific fleet at Pearl Harbor, combined with the recollection of the bombing of civilian and industrial targets in Germany and Britain, led many to the conclusion that America should spread out its targets. The Soviet Union's acquisition of the atomic bomb only made civil defense more urgent. A dispersed population seemed clearly to be a more defensible one, and this factor figured into housing policy and was discussed in the popular press. It seems unlikely that many of those who joined in the rush to the cities' outskirts did so to escape the danger of being bombed. But they did not have to make that decision.

Government mortgage policies perpetuated a kind of actuarial racism. During the immediate postwar years, many cities were just beginning to experience the effects of the other great postwar migration, from the rural South to the urban North. Integrated areas were not perceived as being able to hold their value, so they were declared poor risks and were ineligible for government-guaranteed mortgages. A federal court upheld Levitt's racially discriminating practices. With only a handful of exceptions, the suburbs stayed white. And when blacks moved to the suburbs, it was most often to one of those exceptions that had been allowed to turn black.

Although most of the suburbs started out, and stayed, white, getting away from blacks was not what propelled people to the suburbs. Rather, the move to the suburbs was a fulfillment of the American dream, an expected reward for working hard and coming through many years of hard times.

Unlike previous waves of suburbanization, in which growth followed a railroad line, or even a well-established main highway, the postwar suburbanization happened in a scattered, apparently haphazard way. Despite the rhetoric of those opposed to it, it did not radiate across the countryside from the city center, but rather grew in widely separated patches that were only gradually filled in. For buyers, it was not important to be adjacent to anything in particular, as long as the house was not too long a drive from work. Developers were on the lookout for cheap buildable land that was not too far from other developments, but not so close as to raise the price.

This pattern of suburbanization had another, albeit temporary, advantage for the buyer. His development was surrounded by farms or woods, so even though his own house might be a manufactured object just like his neighbors', he did have the sense of having moved to the country. Most people who moved to suburbia really did get to experience an environment that, for a time at least, retained some rural characteristics.

In New England, for example, suburbs were built in clearings in the forest. Most of these forests grew on long-abandoned farms and were filled with old stone fences and the ruins of barns and wells. Children who lived in such developments were far from being the oppressed, claustrophobic creatures that appear in the anti-suburban literature. In most of America, children could walk to the edge of the development and really find something else. This fact gave rise to one of the most common political phenomena of the age, in which the most recent arrivals became most active in trying to stop further develop-

ment, little realizing that their fellow citizens felt it was *their* houses that had ruined the town.

Inevitably, the arrival of residential development changed the area. Residents realized that farming, while picturesque, is also smelly, and they complained when slow-moving farm equipment slowed traffic on the road. Moreover, farmers found that their tax assessments were rising to reflect the new use for their land, while their income from farming was not. Increasingly, farmers felt pressure to bail out, and they looked for developers to buy and subdivide their land. Depending on the area, this process could take a few months, as was common in Southern California, or as long as a decade. Eventually, though, the blotches in the landscape turned to sprawl. Ultimately, all the farmers would sell and the area would be full.

When the first occupants of the new suburban developments arrived, the land they found rarely matched their dreams. Developments had often sprouted in farmers' fields, but even when they had been cleared from forests, few mature trees were allowed to stand. The economics of building developments precluded saving trees, although a few spindly ones would be planted at the end. Most members of the baby-boom generation grew up without any tree large enough to support a swing. Instead, brightly painted tubular-steel swing and trapeze sets appeared in every yard, and began gradually to rust.

The home buyers had dreams of green lawns, but what they often found was a lot of mud, sometimes crisscrossed with ruts left by construction equipment. From this inauspicious beginning, they sought to create a landscape that was green and picturesque. Their image was of an English park or, similarly, of a golf course. Developments named Country Club Estates did not need to have an actual country club. It was understood that it was simply evoking an image. If the developer had a swampy tract, he could dig and channel and call his development Presidential Lakes. "A vacation that lasts a lifetime begins here," the advertisement would promise.

In the immediate postwar period, almost any suburban house offered at an affordable price was enough to draw buyers, as Levitt's famous lines indicate. These were the Model T's of home building—fairly well-built, practical, identical, single-story boxes, designed in a style that vaguely recalled the modest old frame houses of New England. The Cape Cod style, as it was called, was a standard builder's plan from before World War II, and it, not any self-consciously modern approach, became the standard model for large-scale rationalized housing production at midcentury. At one point Levitt was turning out 150 of them a day.

These were the buildings about which Malvina Reynolds would write the song "Little Boxes." This composition, which may have been the first suburban folk song, was a condemnation of conformity. Suburban houses were "little boxes, on the hillside and they're all made out of ticky tacky . . . and they all look just the same." This song became modestly popular, even in suburbia. But by 1963, when the song was written, it provided an anachronistic view of suburbia. Even in those early postwar developments, which offered only one or two choices of design, people had customized and added on to their houses. And in the early 1950s, housing had turned from a seller's market to one in which the consumer had a lot of choice. And just as the black, thoroughly standardized Model T had made way for cars in various colors, shapes and sizes, so did the prototypical Levitt house make way for a parade of novelties, features and options, even in Levitt developments. Although the song was correct, in the sense that all of the house varieties were basically little boxes, few believed that *they* lived in little boxes. Those were for other people.

After the end of the Korean War in 1953, houses became larger and more lavishly decorated. Rather than offering just one or two models, the typical developer would show four or five, and, like an automobile, each of these was available with various options that would add greater variety, and higher costs. "Enjoy custom community living at project prices," the advertisements promised. "Your happiness is a 'sure thing' at beautiful Haywood Park." The development was still a fact of life, the way to get the most house for the least money. But buyers were encouraged to see the differences among the houses, to make those little individual choices that would show the world that yours was a family of taste and imagination.

What passed for individuality and flair could sometimes take odd shapes and hues. "Pink, orange and turquoise may seem like a weird combination of colors to some people," a 1955 newspaper article began. But that was the combination that won the subject of the article an award for her design skills and a three-week trip to Italy.

The elaborated suburban house of the 1950s and 1960s was unmistakably the developers' creation, and rarely was an architect directly involved. Still, it

Suburbia typically grew in large patches in what used to be countryside, as seen in this 1957 New Jersey view.

did have some highborn parentage. It absorbed and recombined influences both from historic architecture, from the eastern United States back to England and Italy, and from modernism, particularly as it was practiced in California. The single-story ranch-style home swept the country from west to east, while the one-and-a-half-story Cape Cod spread from east to west, and they often ended up as neighbors within the same subdivision. Developers freely mixed and matched both traditional and modern elements in all their houses, and decorating magazines backed this thinking by arguing that the contemporary house was cold without traditional elements and the traditional house was stiff without touches of the contemporary.

There were still a few regional differences about what was meant by traditional. In New England, the trusty Cape Cod could only be made of wood, but in Pennsylvania, a traditional house would be made of stone as first choice, brick as second choice. When the Cape Cod was made of brick, it took on a look it had never had before. Then as you went farther south, there was a significant hangover from *Gone With the Wind*. The little Cape Cod box often got an oversized portico, in which white-painted two-by-fours took the place of classical columns.

Frank Lloyd Wright, America's most celebrated architect, spent most of his very long career designing suburban houses. They ranged from the great sprawling masterpieces he did outside Chicago at the turn of the century to his later, more affordable Usonian prototype houses for the middle class. He sought to introduce dynamism and democracy into a milieu that was characterized by stodginess and elitism. Wright brought the ideal of openness to the suburban house by freeing up the plan and by stressing horizontality and wide windows. The picture window, that most characteristic feature of postwar suburbia, though it represents a bending of his intentions and misunderstanding of his technique, can be traced back to Wright.

The ideal of the horizontal house, which a *Better Homes and Gardens* survey showed was well established nationwide by 1950, had originally been worked out in the Midwest by Wright and the Prairie School. But most people associated it with California, where a well-established modernist tradition had

This East Coast development house boasts a cupola, stone facing, and shutters, but its L-shaped layout is identical to that of tens of thousands of California ranch-style houses.

Frank Lloyd Wright's dream of
beautiful, affordable houses for
all never materialized, but many
of the qualities of his pre–
World War II "Usonian" designs
appeared in postwar houses.
These included walls of windows,
continuous interior spaces, low,
mantel-less, assymetrical fire-
places, indirect lighting,
bracket-mounted shelving, and,
most important of all, a general
air of informality and openness.

merged Wright's ideas with those that came out of Europe during the 1920s and adapted both to the mild climate. From this tradition came the free-flowing open plan, indoor-outdoor living, big windows and light woods. These very open houses did not permit formality or even very much privacy. They opened kitchens to full view and made them an occasion. While architects elsewhere did not take the single-family suburban house very seriously, Californians explored the possibilities through the famous Case Study Houses that were designed and built under the auspices of *Arts & Architecture* magazine.

The high-style modern California houses designed by such influential architects as Richard Neutra and Gregory Ain were demanding to build and to inhabit. They demanded a precision of construction, a richness of material and a level of discipline and neatness from the inhabitants that was uncommon. But the builders of the bulk of suburbia could look and see devices that could be turned into features that would help sell a house. While Neutra commonly used overhanging roofs to shade large windows on the sunny side of the house, developers overlooked the reason and just added the overhang as a bit of Cali-

High-style buildings like Richard Neutra's Bailey House, built in Los Angeles in 1947, influenced many development houses.

fornia styling. And while in the custom-designed houses the largest windows would frame the best view, in a developer's house a similar window would look out on whatever happened to be outside. Most people knew these houses only from illustrations in magazines, so developers did not need to duplicate the experience of being inside these one-of-a-kind creations. They just used a bit of redwood siding and a sliding door to a patio, and they had a California modern house.

One feature of many of the custom-designed houses that made life easier for the developer was the prominent garage which was often the first thing you saw upon arrival. Previously, prestigious houses had had discreet garages, but now obvious garages were acceptable in all price ranges. This was not so much a matter of ostentation as necessity. It was very difficult to hide a garage on a normal suburban lot, and you certainly couldn't do without one.

The California fantasy was very important for developers, no matter where they were building. While a lot of people moved to California during this period, polls showed that millions more wanted to. It conjured up powerful dreams of informal living, ideal weather and movie-star glamour. Even in Cape Cod houses, one might find something described as "a Hollywood closet," which was presumably large enough for many changes of costume.

The picture window originated in high-style houses, but it quickly became a standard feature of suburban tract houses.

Still, it probably makes the most sense to see suburban houses, not in terms of historic or modernist designs, but rather as variations of the developer's box that they were at heart. This is true even though the major effect in styling houses for developers was to break up the typical boxy profile. The solution was either to make it longer and lower in feeling, following the example of automobiles, or to present it as a group of different shapes, planes, materials, colors and textures. Most such effort was expended on the front of the house. The shingled, wood-sided or red-brick front gave way to façades that had stone-faced bases, strips of windows with bright-colored siding and sections of "rainbow brick" or contrasting shingles. Front doors were often highly decorated with wide rectangular panels and a classical or patriotic motif at the center. Garage doors could match or contrast.

Small triangular elements, evoking unconscious memories of classical pediments, began to appear over picture windows. This was an opportunity to put in the siding diagonally in order to get another shape onto the front of the house. Builders cantilevered second stories a few inches over the first, or recessed one side of the house a few inches back from the other, in order to increase the number of planes visible on the front of a house and increase its apparently rambling quality. Rambling was good, because it promised size, an attribute the house itself could not always offer. The proliferation of planes in the front of a house afforded the additional opportunity to make each one seem different, by using contrasting colors, materials, textures or patterns. While two-toning was started by the automobile industry, the variety of colors, materials and textures available on housefronts allowed even more startling effects than were possible on a car.

Such domestic grandeur was only for public consumption, however. When you walked around to the side and back of the house, the walls were generally

The modern house was long
and low, asymmetrical and
dynamic, and it welcomed and
honored the automobile. It was
a place of contrasts, where
horizontal bands of stone played
against vertical and horizontal
siding, often in different colors—
except in the back, where
everything was plain and boxy.

entirely flat and covered with only one color of shingles or siding. Even though many homeowners placed high value on their backyards, they presumably did not sit out there and look at the boring backs of their houses. Often they looked at the boring backs of other people's houses.

The most often remarked-upon feature of the suburban house is the picture window, which made its way into virtually every style and price of house built during the period. It originated as a way for developers to make their tiny postwar houses feel a little more spacious than nine hundred or so square feet. These windows captured the public imagination, however, and were built into very spacious houses and installed in older houses to make them seem brighter and up-to-date.

Scorners of suburbia noted that the picture window was most often placed at the front of the house, where it afforded the householder a view of other houses much like his own, and cut down on his privacy besides. If the picture window were on the back, however, it might grant a view of a disheveled backyard, and a neighbors' as well.

It made sense for the picture window to be in front, because it provided virtually the only opportunity for the occupants of the house to enjoy the front yard. Although it went largely unused for sitting or any kind of family activity, the front of the house served as its face and received a lot of attention. The best trees, and especially flowering shrubs, were planted in the front yard. The front entrance would often have an ornamental lamppost, to welcome visitors. The car would be sitting in the driveway, a mark of prosperity and mobility. It is even likely that the front lawn got that extra measure of fertilizer and careful attention that would make it, as the advertising said, "the envy of the neighborhood." Householders policed their half-acreage with herbicidal "killer canes," to banish dandelions and make their lawns ever more carpetlike. And in this tableau, the picture window was not only a way of looking out on one's achievement but also a way of looking in. Often, it framed a lamp and other decorative items that were purchased specifically for display there. And it also framed family life, which was visible, although not often intelligible, through the always open draperies.

By 1955, it was obvious that developers could not simply appear to be breaking up the box. They had to do so. The reason was not a matter of style but of economics. Suburban land was becoming increasingly expensive, home buyers sought more and more space, and suburban communities were passing legislation that required houses to be constructed a specified minimum distance from their various property lines. They had to get more house on a smaller lot.

The obvious solution was to build two-story houses, but the FHA study of buyer preferences showed that only 16 percent wanted a two-story house, compared with 74 percent who wanted a single story. That was an overwhelming preference that could not be ignored. The challenge was to make a two-story house that wasn't two stories, and the solution was the split level.

The basic idea of the split level is to put part of the living space—either the kitchen and dining room or the bedrooms—into what would otherwise be basement. Half a level above that would be the front door of the house and the living room. And half a level above that, over the erstwhile basement, were the rest of the rooms. Sometimes, a sub-living-room level would serve as the garage. The advantage of this configuration for the builder was that it made the basement habitable, and he could gain extra living space without a lot more construction. Because there was nothing above the living room, he could shift the gable to the front of the house and let the room go to the roof in the form of a "cathedral ceiling," another marketable feature. The shape of the split level is two boxes, side by side, which made its construction only a bit more complex than that of a ranch or a Cape Cod.

For the buyer, the split level was supposed to be more convenient than an ordinary two-story house, because it is easier to walk up a few steps than a whole flight of stairs. This reasoning seems questionable, at best. The real advantage for the buyer was that the builder was able to pass along some of his construction savings and offer more house for the money.

At the beginning of 1954, hardly anyone had heard of the split level, but by the spring of 1955, it was universally understood to be the latest thing in houses. Developers advertised "We have split levels!" as a come-on to get people to look at all their houses. And while the split-level mania of 1955 has long since passed, these houses remain a fixture of the suburban landscape and are still being built today.

The split level was not really a new style of house. Rather it was a new product. It differed from the ranch much as a station wagon differed from a four-door sedan. The split level could be made available in colonial outfitting or antebellum plantation or California contemporary. Even though Henry VIII might never have recognized it, the split level was even decked out in what became known as English Tudor—perhaps to distinguish it from the Ford Tudor sedan.

The split level was the most successful new product to come from the housing industry in the mid-1950s, and it spawned others. One that had a measure of success was the so-called raised ranch. This sounds like a contradiction in terms, much like the so-called hardtop convertible car, which was popular around the same time. Populuxe nomenclature embraced such contradiction because it was designed to convince consumers they could have it all. Modern and traditional, showy and tasteful, machine-made and craftsmanlike, all these could be reconciled in the same household, sometimes in the same object.

The raised ranch, or bi-level as it was sometimes called, was nothing more than a two-story house with bedrooms occupying the basement level and with the main rooms of the house upstairs. You entered from between the two floors and went up a few steps to the living room. On the outside, two-toning was used heavily to accent the horizontality of the upper, "ranch," portion of the house. This could be a light or bright color, and it would frequently cantilever slightly over a darker-colored base floor. The final effect was often extremely

Houses strove for informality and openness. They were supposed to be fun to live in. Portable appliances in the family room cut down on trips to the kitchen. In the family room, knotty-pine paneling was the material of choice.

Tile and bathroom fixtures in bright, often contrasting, colors made bathrooms lively and smoothly modern. There was no more excuse for an old-fashioned bathroom than for an old-fashioned kitchen.

ungainly, but one thing was accomplished: it did not look like a two-story house. Instead it looked like a ranch-style house that had fallen out of the air and landed atop something else.

Additions to the homebuilders' product lines also included new kinds of spaces and new uses for rooms. The most important of these was the "family room." It began life as a playroom or rumpus room, often to be found in the basement. By the mid-1950s, it was starting to turn into a second, more heavily used living room, and by 1960, the hearth and the television set had made the move. The living room increasingly became more formal and traditional in its furnishings, while the family room had a more contemporary feel and was furnished with more durable, knockabout furniture. The coming of the family room was merely a throwback to the middle-class Victorian house, where the front parlor was rarely used and another room emerged for actual living. The magazines were, to an extent, correct in their description of the family room as "the newest room in the house, and also the oldest."

In some parts of the South, the family room emerged as the Great Room, a term that contains a hint of baronial splendor. But the idea of the family room was more potent. It reminded people of what they cared about, what they hoped their house would strengthen. "When Jim comes home," said a young wife in a 1954 advertisement for National Homes, a prefabricator, "our family room seems to draw us closer together." With its pine paneling, its brick fireplace and comfortable sofas and chairs, the family room exuded coziness.

A similar idea that had a significant impact was the "living kitchen," which came along at the end of the 1950s. In early postwar houses, kitchens were small, so they were marketed as highly efficient technological creations. Later, people had larger families, and they were buying larger houses. The living kitchen responded to a need for space to serve ordinary meals to the family, but it was also a way for the manufacturers of kitchen materials to fight for a bigger share of the construction budget and keep the money from being spent on more sofas and carpeting in the family room. "There is a definite trend toward making mother a member of the family again," exclaimed a 1959 Formica advertisement, and the living kitchen, complete with husband and children sitting around, was sold as a benefit for the woman. In advertisements, of course, everyone is harmonious and well behaved. The living kitchen never made the transition from a marketing term into the general vocabulary, as the family room did, but kitchens did grow larger and more habitable.

One innovation that never caught on was the "living garage." This concept, which was touted by *House & Garden* as one of the important trends of 1958, was based on the premise that cars were becoming ever more beautiful and people should have the opportunity to enjoy them more. The garage was to receive a new tile floor, be decorated with house plants and furnished with tables and chairs and the kind of furniture you might find on a porch or even in a living kitchen. For a fraction of the cost of adding a new room, the magazine said, you could get all the advantages of extra space and enjoy your car

In 1958, *House & Garden* predicted that people would be spending more time with their beautiful new cars in "living garages" like this one.

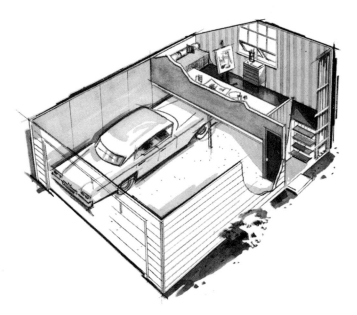

too. Consumers during the Populuxe era bought a lot of dubious ideas. It is reassuring to see that they were able to draw the line somewhere, and the living garage, with its threat of death by carbon monoxide poisoning, was beyond what they were willing to accept.

Design and Styling

"At General Electric," Ronald Reagan used to say when he was the company's corporate spokesman, "progress is our most important product."

Clearly, GE was not coming up with a better light bulb every day or every year, or even working on doing so. The manifestation of progress on, say, a television set might involve moving the controls from below the screen to above the screen and designing them in such a way that the television resembled a friendly robot. GE's brand of progress was also manifested in the marketing of new products for which nobody had been clamoring but for which a market niche might be carved out. The electric frying pan and the four-slice toaster might not have advanced civilization, but they did advance the small-appliance industry.

No, the most significant aspect of the slogan was its downplaying of the actual products in favor of a far vaguer promise that the sum total of GE's research, manufacturing and marketing would constitute progress. Like all other mass manufacturers, GE had no interest in having its customers become attached and devoted to one particular product. Instead, they sought to create an aura of confidence. They wanted their customers to be pleased with their existing products, but not so contented that they would not be tempted to replace them when the new, improved model, with many new and exciting features, was introduced. For GE, as for other large consumer companies, production was the paramount goal. Products were important only insofar as they could be made and sold at a price people would pay and the machinery would be kept in motion.

This system did not evolve during the Populuxe era. It dates back at least to the 1920s, when Henry Ford, who had designed the Model T and stuck with it year after year, lost out to General Motors, which introduced color, choice and frequent change. But the pace of "improvement" surely quickened in the Populuxe years as products received massive cosmetic changes even if they were really remaining the same. In retrospect, some of these improvements seem comical. In 1957, *Look* ran an article about the "new early American look," contrasting it with the "early American" of, say, 1956. The Populuxe years surely brought a heightening of the mythology and fantasy used to sell products. In making a purchase, you bought into a way of life. Americans had begun by taming an entire continent of wilderness. World dominion had come virtually unsought, and now Americans, a people at the vanguard of the quest of mankind, were about to step off the planet and confront the universe itself, if those pesky Russians didn't foil their plans.

And at the same time that Americans believed themselves to be moving toward national realization, they were also moving toward self-realization. Individual citizens had, they were told, freedom to express themselves and live on a level of comfort of which all mankind, up to that moment, could scarcely have dared to dream. Overstated and naïve as this sense of destiny seems today, there were grounds for optimism. A belief in material progress drove the generally robust economy of these years. And this economy proved capable of producing products that a great many people could buy and enjoy. Material democracy had been achieved not through any arts-and-crafts utopia, or through a socialist forced redistribution of wealth, but rather through the workings of big business and its expertise in making people feel good about its products. Progress was not merely an abstraction, but an array of goods that could be touched, switched on, photographed, improved and fantasized about.

Though this was a great age for having things, it was not a good time for people who loved fine things. Populuxe connoisseurship is a contradiction in terms. Virtually all products were sold with the understanding that something better would be coming out soon. Populuxe managed to reconcile the selling of many products with the ideal of traveling light. You did not have to worry about what you would pass on to your children, because they would have things unimaginably better than yours. The important issue was convenience, here and now. Service, not durability, was paramount. Today, most collectors will look for objects that go against the grain of the period and reflect privilege and craftsmanship. Such collectors look for the merits of objects in themselves, while in the Populuxe era objects were simply a means to an end. Paradoxically, many of the semi-handmade products that today's collectors prize sought to celebrate the promise of the machine. Meanwhile, the machine was delivering; nearly all of the characteristic objects of the time were machine-made. Machines had difficulty turning out products that had the elegance of the machine-inspired work of 1920s European modernists, but they could produce a wealth of products that symbolized the promise of modern American life.

To the dismay of many tastemakers, these products were often bogus antiques. Most critics of Populuxe taste tended to project themselves back in time and see themselves in the role of the happy few who had fine things, rather than that of the majority who had little or nothing. The average consumer of the 1950s was, by contrast, quite eager to possess machine-made products which carried the look and associations of handcrafted products that had once been available only to the highly privileged. Manufacturers ransacked different historical periods and different cultures to come up with this year's anachronisms. There was, for example, a marketing push for something called Basque Provincial, though it never caught on. The most successful reproductions were derived from the American past, especially that of the colonial and federal periods. These were associated with the nation's beginnings and with a period of graceful, though not fussy or ornate, styles. Somewhat incongruously, Early American furniture was vaguely associated with the opening of the frontier and with the Old West, a fascination that dominated the prime-time television schedule for most of the late 1950s. The real look of that period was Victorian—dark, heavy and solid, although it is unlikely that very many such pieces could be piled into a covered wagon. Victorian designs were shunned by the mass market and serious collectors during the Populuxe years, even though the two eras had something in common. Both brought an explosion in the number and variety of things to own and the number of people who were able to own them.

Some who cared about fine design and well-made products felt that democracy was on trial during this period and that it was failing miserably. They looked at the landscape of subdivision houses, the gaudy cars in the showrooms, the profusion of overweight furniture standing on tiny legs, and despaired that aristocracy had done things so much better. "We have yet to prove that a democracy can produce a beautiful environment," wrote the architect Edward Durell Stone in a 1959 article, "The Case Against the Tailfin Age." Stone, one of the few architects to design in the spirit of Populuxe and achieve widespread acclaim, even condemned the ranch-style house as "a good excuse for laziness: it is transparently easier to feed the children in the back yard—like ranch hands—than it is to have them seated at a table behaving like potentially civilized adults." This is, in part, the old complaint that newfound wealth does not buy good manners or good taste, at least in the first generation. But the amount of new money around in the Populuxe era was staggering, and it changed the quality even of what was available to the rich. The affluent could buy symbols of their wealth, but they could not buy the materials and craftsmanship to which they had been accustomed.

The standard was, of course, that of the marketplace. Products were judged not by how well they were made, or how well they did their jobs, but by how well they sold. Indeed, the American tradition of industrial design is based on just this premise. In contrast with the tradition of craftsmanship exemplified by William Morris and his followers, and with the ideology of technical expression that arose with the Bauhaus and European modernism, American industrial design has been concerned most of all with inducing consumers to accept, understand and use a product. Just looking at the backgrounds of the generation that invented American industrial design during the 1930s gives a sense of what their clients were looking for. Raymond Loewy started out as a fashion illustrator. Henry Dreyfuss, who became the chief exponent of scientific rigor in design, started out as a stage designer, and he got into the field when Macy's asked him if he could repackage some of their products to make them sell better. Norman Bel Geddes also came from the theater. In 1940, the designer Harold Van Doren, in discussing the appropriateness of streamlining products that don't move, wrote: "If it helps to sell merchandise, that should go a long way toward justifying its use."

Because American industrial designers worked directly with the producers of products, they became much more sophisticated about how industrial processes work than were the Europeans who were the most influential commentators on living with the machine. Le Corbusier, for example, argued that machines functionally resolve themselves into combinations of simple geometric forms that are beautiful in themselves, a conclusion one might draw from looking at the mechanically optimistic paintings of Léger. Le Corbusier's observation was true of the relatively primitive airplanes, automobiles and industrial machinery to which he alluded, but by the late 1920s it was becoming apparent that sound engineering was no guarantee of beauty. How something looks is quite different from how well it works, which is, in turn, different from how it feels to use it. A mechanically functional device can work less well if it intimidates the user.

Two Henry Dreyfuss designs from the 1950s: the plastic Western Electric telephone and the round Honeywell thermostat.

The most famous instance of this phenomenon was Raymond Loewy's 1929 redesign of the Gestetner duplicating machine. Although it worked just fine when Loewy first saw it, its visual complexity was intimidating, its overall look was ungainly, and the parts that stuck out snagged clothing and were easy to trip over. Secretaries perceived it not as a convenience but as an imposition that was studded with booby traps. Loewy simply designed a new housing for the machine, covering up parts that did not need to be visible in everyday use, smoothing out the lines and making it look less formidable. The design was sold, virtually unchanged, until well into the 1960s. Loewy later joked that a design that is *too* successful puts the designer out of business because he cannot get repeat work. Actually, Loewy designed a number of other products for Gestetner, but his remark had a lot of truth to it.

Loewy, Dreyfuss and the others served corporations during the 1930s as engineers of the emotions, experts in making the connection between people and machines. They also became known in the popular press as oracles of the future. But their insights into the way people felt about and used industrial products did not have a strong impact on everyday life because there was not a lot of buying during the Depression. After World War II, however, manufacturers began to offer a tremendous variety of products that were so sophisticated in their operation that even the avid *Popular Mechanics* reader would have a lot of trouble knowing how each product worked and how each could be repaired. If markets for such products were to expand, manufacturers would have to induce quite a lot of blind faith on the part of the consumer. Manufacturers had to sell confidence before they could sell the product, and the appearance of the product could contribute strongly to such a feeling. If potential buyers were to think too much about what was happening inside, they might be frightened away. Thus did the reel-type power mower, a machine that combined a fully exposed and sputtering gasoline engine with exposed swirling blades, give way to the rotary mower, which generally managed to package all of this violence neatly and keep the blades somewhat more safely out of sight. Rotary lawn mowers were often shown being used by smiling grandmothers, young women and cheerful children to downplay fears of mechanical complexity and chopped-off fingers. Because market surveys indicated that women were playing an increasing role in purchasing decisions, particularly for items used around the house, mechanical qualities were played down and convenience was emphasized. The products were not machines in themselves but components of a way of life. GE did not sell stoves. It sold progress, and stoves were an important part of that.

It is possible to trace the evolution of this approach in the changing image

Dangerous blades were hidden and covered in the rotary lawn mower, so that it would be safe even for a woman to use.

of the ideal kitchen. During the early 1950s, when families were still catching up after the war, a modern kitchen was simply an old-fashioned kitchen to which many new appliances had been added. Each of the appliances was slightly streamlined. Each stood on its own, a separate piece of machinery. The kitchen table often had a wooden base and an enameled metal top, and oak chairs had given way to plastic-upholstered, tubular-metal cantilevered chairs, derived from those developed by Marcel Breuer at the Bauhaus during the 1920s.

At the dawn of the Populuxe era, roundness was out as a visual style, so appliances became squarer, or "sheer," as they were called at the time. But there was an even more fundamental change of perception. The appliances were no longer seen as objects in the kitchen. Rather, they *were* the kitchen. Modern life was close to inconceivable without them. Thus, appliances were increasingly built into kitchens. Ovens went up on walls while burners interrupted expanses of counters. Dishwashers nestled next to the sink. At first, the imagery partook of the laboratory. The environment was so clean and uninterrupted that even cupboard doors weren't allowed to have handles. Everything was recessed, hidden or built-in. Women were hailed as household engineers at the same time that they were reassured that they did not have to know much more about the sophisticated machinery they were using than how to turn it on. Magazines were far more likely to refer to household appliances as "conveniences," or even "servants," than as the machines they so clearly were. The kitchen table had a light-colored Formica top that coordinated with that of the rest of the kitchen. The table had tubular-metal legs, like the chairs, which were four-legged rather than cantilevered. Their padding was more generous, and their vinyl covering either matched the tabletop, provided a vibrant contrast or, because they were two-toned, did both. Nearly indestructible plastic dishes were available in a palette as vivid and artificial as that used on the table and chairs.

In the early 1960s, imagery from the dining room began to come back into

Paul McCobb's "Planner" furniture and George Nelson's bubble lamps were certified by the Museum of Modern Art as "good design."

the kitchen. The top of the kitchen table might still be Formica, but it would have a walnut grain. The coverings of the chairs were more subdued, or the chairs might even be made of wood. Throughout the room, warmer tones appeared, along with frilly curtains, colorful fabrics, spice racks, canisters and other old-fashioned homey elements. By this time, the appliances were so basic to the operation of the kitchen as to become almost invisible. Although the bright pink and turquoise appliances of the mid-1950s had not been nearly as popular as cars of the same color, kitchen machinery in earth tones, such as green and bronze, did well during the 1960s because they were seen less as appliances than as part of an overall decorating scheme. Appliances no longer had to be dramatized; they were thoroughly domesticated. And the stage was set for the transition from the homemaker/glamour girl who bought Wonder Bread to the working mother who made her own bread.

The changing imagery of everyday life required new objects, even when the old appliances and furniture still did an adequate job. This new perception of objects as part of a way of life rather than as tools for carrying out a particular task required that design be thought about in a whole new way. The individual object became less important. Design for mass production involved more sociological insight than technical expertise or aesthetic intention. It is likely that even the famous Good Design shows at the Museum of Modern Art, which were trying to fight this trend, ended up being a part of it. They were intended to spotlight well-made, visually graceful objects for everyday use. Their effect was to let a small group of consumers signal that their households had the approval of the Museum of Modern Art.

"What else does it do besides work?" was the consumer's question then, and perhaps now as well. What distinguishes the Populuxe approach is the strong accent given the psychological expressions, the naïve celebration of possessions which disappeared as the objects being celebrated became commonplace. Objects responded less to needs than to moods, and the environment of which they were a part was seen to be changing every day. There was

American consumption was a wonder of the world. Here, a German delegation examines an American refrigerator

no incentive for the designer to try to create a classic because it would have to be thrown aside anyway. Echoing the famous Horatio Greenough–Louis Sullivan slogan, "Form follows function," Edgar Kaufmann, Jr., organizer of the Museum of Modern Art's Good Design shows, noted, "Style follows sales." And although the Modern continues to act as a connoisseur of industrial design, collecting objects it considers to be exemplary, it has long since given up the effort to be the kind of tastemaker in everyday artifacts that it is in painting, photography or architecture.

The very nature of *things* had changed. An unprecedented distribution of disposable income had created a disposable world. Use it once and throw it away was the promise of many consumer products. The concept of planned obsolescence, pioneered by General Motors during the 1920s, was commonly understood, and accepted. Artifacts were specifically designed not to last. The object was not the object. Rather, the goal was production, sales and continued economic activity. And faced with a declining group of buyers, change, or the illusion of change, was the most important inducement to get people to buy. This, in turn, demanded styling and restyling. A product might not really be new and improved, but as long as it looked different, and exciting, it had a better chance of being bought.

By traditional standards, this approach to making and using things was enormously wasteful. It did not merely encourage but depended on the dis-

Appliances evolved from big boxes in the kitchen to efficient, square-edged, laboratory-like objects to assertive built-ins, before disappearing into an overall decorating scheme. Plastic laminate table tops and vinyl seat covers permitted colorful dinette sets.

carding of valuable materials, the scrapping of things that still worked. Throughout the first half of the 1950s, intellectuals condemned American behavior as wasteful, often comparing it with that of the French housewife going to the store with her net bag that she reuses again and again. This was all very picturesque, but the question arose: why were so many more Americans well off than the thriftier Europeans. Indeed, Europe was developing an ever larger class that viewed itself as proletarian and essentially in opposition to the economic system, while in America even such traditional industrial employees as automobile workers defined themselves as solidly middle class.

By the latter half of the decade, the argument had swung in the other direction. The economic commentator Peter Drucker argued, for example, that the apparent wastefulness was actually a form of subsidy which allowed those at the lower end of the economic ladder to partake of the same pleasures as everyone else. Thus, a person who wanted a stylish and exciting new car would usually discard an old car that still ran well but was no longer in style. A poorer person could then buy it used for less than it was really worth. New styling had both increased the value of the new car and lowered the value of the used car. If people kept cars as long as they were useful, the argument goes, many people would never be able to afford a car. But by providing other reasons to buy a new car, styling created a subsidy for the less affluent that made automobile ownership almost universal.

Even George Nelson, who as design director of Herman Miller served as the patron of furniture classics and designed a few of them himself, eventually came around to a variation of this argument. "Rapid large-scale consumption," he wrote, "certainly accelerates the replacement of plant and tools, and thus renewal is at a higher technological level. Does an industry-based society reach a point where the highest efficiency is reached through what superficially appears to be waste?" He seemed to think that it does, although an element of doubt lingered, and he was far from pleased with the quality of many of the physical results of this kind of thinking: "Most current dwellings are uniformly tasteless and thus inoffensive, the architectural equivalents of a can of pressed ham."

There is something undeniably absurd in the premise that as long as people keep buying items they don't need, the economy will prosper. It smells of perpetual motion and other physical impossibilities. "If we all just go out and buy a parakeet," said one commentator, "everything will be all right." The parakeet was a perfect Populuxe pet, which was friendlier and had more fashionably colored feathers than its competitor the canary, and an additional feature, its alleged ability to talk. The remark was meant to be satirical, but it was used nonetheless by the editor of a furniture trade magazine to chastise his readers for not having come up with the kind of unnecessary products that he felt were essential to the industry's prosperity. Whether something was unnecessary was not really the point, of course. The crucial challenge was to integrate the product into the customer's idea of the way life ought to be.

Eero Saarinen's "tulip" series for Knoll (1956).

The celebration of the production and sales process at the expense of the products proved doubly painful to many who were, like Nelson, advocates of modern furniture design. The postwar period was a kind of golden age of American design. Charles and Ray Eames produced a series of designs that proved to be classics, as did Charles Eames's sometime collaborator Eero Saarinen. Harry Bertoia's wire chairs and Nelson's "coconut" chair and storage walls were also familiar parts of the American landscape. Between them, Knoll and Herman Miller seemed to be making possible the creation of a distinctly American modernism in furniture. Like Bauhaus and most other prewar European modernist designs, these pieces sought to reflect a machine-based society. But the European pieces were primarily formal experiments, handcrafted objects which sought to question the familiar images of particular pieces, and they were concerned most of all with structure. The chair, for example, ceased to be a thing with four legs, a seat and a back. Instead, the seat would be cantilevered, or the seat and back would become tension members of a formidable structure. Some sought primarily to be sculptures that could be sat on. Of the Europeans, however, only Alvar Aalto had designed pieces in terms of the processes by which they would be made. And Aalto worked only in laminated wood.

The postwar American designs, by contrast, followed the native method of close integration of design, marketing and production. And they were designed to take advantage of new materials and new technologies. Perhaps the definitive example was the foam and molded fiberglass "womb" chair, designed by Eero Saarinen and introduced by Knoll in 1948. This bucket seat proved to be the prototype for a great many variations on the theme of a molded sculptural seat standing on frail metal legs. "Ass trays," Frank Lloyd Wright called them, but they started turning up everywhere. One of Saarinen's own variations was adopted for use throughout the mammoth General Motors Technical Center, which Saarinen designed. The connection of the legs to the seat was the most difficult technical problem associated with the chair, but even after this was solved the incongruity of legs and seat was the most difficult aesthetic problem. It was even more serious in Eames's similar naked plastic bucket of 1949. Yet both designs appeared self-evidently to be a whole new way to make a chair. The womb chair became so familiar an icon of the modern that Norman Rockwell immortalized it as a hiding place for a somewhat guilty father trying to escape the rest of his family as they go off to church. He could have hidden himself more effectively in a winged chair, perhaps, but the womb chair very quietly embodied the father's break with tradition. Ironically, although the chair's scrawny metal legs were probably its least successful feature, this was the element that furniture manufacturers adopted to give their lines a contem-

Norman Rockwell used Saarinen's "womb" chair as a guilt-ridden father's refuge. Right: George Nelson's "coconut" chair for Herman Miller (1956).

porary look. Eames had earlier used such legs on his innovative, doubly curved plywood chairs, which proved to be the inspiration for the furniture of classrooms, offices and waiting rooms for decades, and most other serious designers used them also. Later, Saarinen designed the "tulip" series of chairs in which the molded seat stands on a white metal pedestal, so that the entire chair had a visual, if not material, unity. It solved the problem of what Saarinen had termed "the slum of legs," but by that time, this so-called slum had taken on prestige of its own.

The designs of Eames, Saarinen, Nelson, Bertoia and others were generally informal. They sought to be light and comfortable. They were realistic about the body and did not make it conform to a particular sculptural form, but rather let the furniture mirror the shapes and motions of the body on the surfaces where contact would be made. This furniture was, therefore, a bit more ungainly than the canonical 1920s modernist forms, but it was closer to modernist ideals of practical, affordable, machine-made furniture. It was extremely influential, and it did turn up in people's lives, if not necessarily in their houses. Moreover, it conveyed a sense of the new and the dynamic.

But the work of the innovative American designers did not ultimately add up to the kind of environment in which people actually lived. This had something to do with the nature of the furniture industry itself, which was divided into many small companies, most of them making only chests or upholstered goods or metal furniture. The new furniture used combinations of materials and technologies that most manufacturers defined as being outside of their particular business. And while Knoll and Herman Miller did pursue the residential market in their early years, their standards of construction and the prices they had to charge made their products much more attractive to the corporate and institutional market, where the durability they offered was more in demand. And the immediate and widespread acceptance of modern American furniture for institutional uses probably worked against its use in the home. The Populuxe house was viewed as being an island of individuality, a refuge from the world at large. If a chair could be found at the school library, it probably would not be found in the home.

Nevertheless, a lot of modern and contemporary furniture was sold for the home. Much of this had a superficial similarity to the sort of thing Eames was doing, but it generally left out the technological innovation. The commercial-grade furniture, called "borax" and "waterfall" in the trade, was made essentially the same way whether it was labeled "contemporary," "traditional" or "Early American." Today, one can look at the advertising of a big company like Kroehler and not be able to tell the traditional from the modern without a label. Yet manufacturers offered immense apparent variety. In 1957, one average-sized furniture manufacturer offered twenty different styles of standard sofas, three styles of sectionals, eighteen styles of love seats and thirty-nine upholstered chairs, each available in seventeen different qualities of fabric, each available in a dozen or more colors and patterns. You could buy anything you wanted, as long as it was conventional.

Contemporary, modern, traditional, classic, early American. More or less the same furniture was varied to appeal to different tastes.

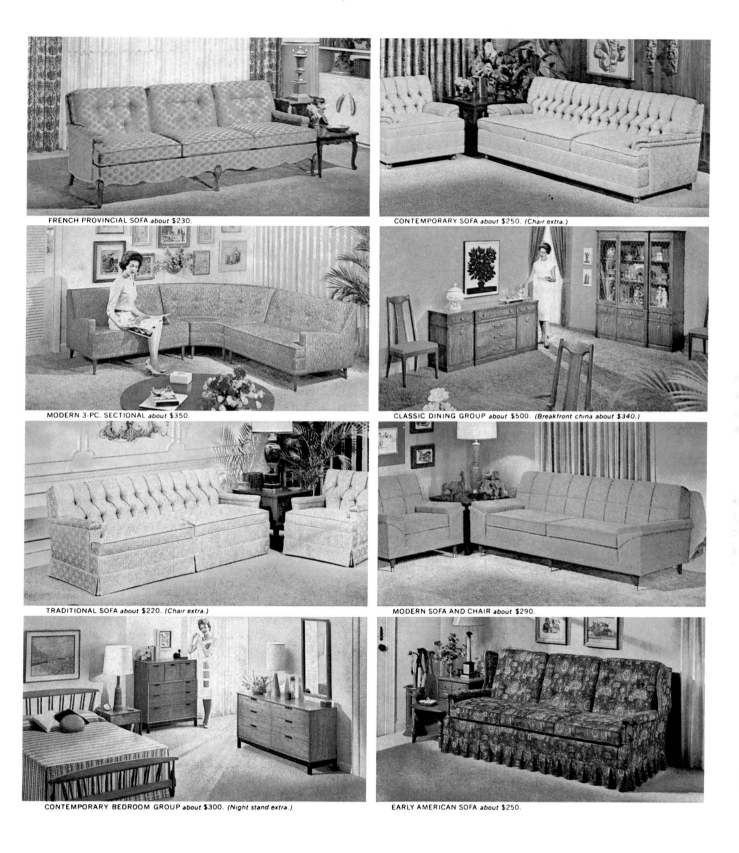

FRENCH PROVINCIAL SOFA *about $230.*

CONTEMPORARY SOFA *about $250. (Chair extra.)*

MODERN 3-PC. SECTIONAL *about $350.*

CLASSIC DINING GROUP *about $500. (Breakfront china about $340.)*

TRADITIONAL SOFA *about $220. (Chair extra.)*

MODERN SOFA AND CHAIR *about $290.*

CONTEMPORARY BEDROOM GROUP *about $300. (Night stand extra.)*

EARLY AMERICAN SOFA *about $250.*

Pole lamps were flexible, modern, and almost everywhere.

The word "modern" was often used for furniture that was a bit more daring in design, a bit more fashionable, than the furniture designated as "contemporary." Confusingly, the terms were often used in a different way, with "modern" used as an antonym for "formal," describing an attitude toward living and room arrangement that could embrace traditional pieces as well as those that were consciously contemporary. But both definitions of "modern" implied an aspiration to lightness, both in color and in line. Lighter woods predominated, even in Early American.

Contemporary tables and small decorative objects such as ashtrays took on dynamic asymmetrical forms, such as boomerang or palette shapes, while larger contemporary objects tended to be boxy. There were no moldings, and thin, slightly splayed, round metal or metal-footed wooden legs were almost universal. The most characteristic piece of modern lighting was the pogo-stick pole lamp, a painted metal rod with spring mounts at either end to attach it to both floor and ceiling. Mounted along the pole were several lamps, each with a utilitarian bullet-shaped metal shade, that could be turned to focus light where it was needed. Not too surprisingly, this was not the invention of the furniture industry, but rather of a Connecticut photographer who rigged one up in his studio and found that people liked his lamp better than his pictures. It was a design that appealed to sophisticated and naïve tastes equally, because it had visual lightness, flexibility, convenience and novelty. The bullet-shaded lamps could also be found attached to flexible metal necks on desks and tables, and even in mobilelike balanced fixtures.

The other feature of contemporary design which was found in both high-style and mainstream homes was wall-mounted shelving, either attached to

Visually light shelving grids were another new kind of furniture.

the wall or featuring thin metal stanchions. Several decorating books published at the time identified such shelving, along with what was termed "the color revolution," as the decorative touch by which the era would be known. Like the pole lamp, this shelving appeared serviceable and almost weightless, with an industrial quality that was not particularly overbearing. The shelves defined a grid on which all sorts of objects, from books to record players to clusters of African sculpture, family pictures or souvenir bric-a-brac, could be placed. The grid was an important motif, one that was identified both with the walls of new downtown office buildings and with the paintings of Mondrian, whose influence had trickled down to cigarette advertisements and the decoration of kitchen cabinets. The grid underlay modular furniture in which desks, cabinets and chests of drawers were set into a wall of shelving. This was a fashion which could be found all the way from the richly austere executive

George Nelson's comprehensive storage system (1958) was adaptable for home or office.

suite to the cheap motel, where all the shelves except the ones that held the suitcase and the television were usually empty. In the home, however, the shelving presented a light framework on which to place an array of shapes and colors. Homeowners were constantly being exhorted to express themselves, and placing knickknacks on such shelf-filled walls provided a fairly inexpensive way to do so.

Nothing so satisfactory or widely popular appeared in the mass market for contemporary upholstered pieces. Mostly, they were identifiable as contemporary by the presence of square corners everywhere. Even the arm of a chair would appear as either a huge upholstered block or a narrow remnant of an arm. Sectional sofas, which fit into corners with large square tables in between, were most commonly produced in contemporary styles, and they were marketed as embodiments of the flexibility required by modern living. The thing that prevented contemporary upholstered furniture from showing a truly modern line was its conventional wooden box and coil spring construction. It stood on thin legs, but the chair or sofa itself inevitably looked overweight. While Nelson and Saarinen dealt with this problem by using thin layers of foam and unconventional structures, the mainstream furniture makers didn't deal with the issue at all. They simply declared that this is what modern furniture looked like.

It is instructive to contrast one of the classic American modern designs of the period, the Eames 1956 rosewood and leather lounge chair and ottoman, with its generic Populuxe equivalent, the reclining easy chair. The Eames chair is a truly splendid embodiment of the idea of modern personal luxury. It is a kind of throne, one that makes use of very rich materials and allows the body to recline, to slouch, to lean back or pull forward. It is a tour de force of functionalist design, conceived not as a chair in the traditional sense of seat, back and legs, but rather as a series of curved surfaces that give the body support at key places. This chair was expensive to make and expensive to buy, which helps explain why it did not achieve widespread popularity when it first became available. Moreover, Herman Miller did not offer any of its line through the retail market. General Motors styling chief Harley Earl was among those who special-ordered one, though he replaced the dark leather covering with orange Naugahyde.

Nevertheless, the tremendous impact it had during the 1970s, when the baby-boom generation started buying knockoffs of the Eames lounge to furnish their apartments, raises the question of why the same kind of thing did not happen sooner after the chair was introduced. Its problem may have been its very thronelike quality. It claims a large part of any room, and it does not fit easily into any particular look. And although the Populuxe ethos encouraged self-indulgence, the Eames lounge chair possibly called too much attention to the search for comfort. (During the 1976 presidential debates, an Eames lounge chair was placed next to each of the podiums, to allow one candidate to rest while the other was talking. Neither candidate ever dared sit in his chair, even when one of the debates was interrupted for twenty-seven minutes by a sound system failure.)

Even high-style furniture, such as this Edward Wormley sofa, was sold with space-age fantasy.

The Populuxe recliner was just as ungainly though not quite as large as the Eames chair. And while the Eames lounge chair conveys an image of lounging even when nobody is in it, the empty recliner stands in a more dignified upright position. The history of the reclining chair is a very long one. Recognizable American forebears date to the beginning of the nineteenth century, and the Winterthur Museum has an 1810 New England example that is functionally the same as the 1950s La-Z-Boy, foldout footrest and all. William Morris did a lot to make the recliner respectable, although only the backs of his chairs were adjustable. Late-nineteenth-century American models were frightening contraptions, with gears and ratchets sticking out the back. But during the Populuxe era, the recliner was transformed from a gimmick to a respectable part of the household.

As with so many other products of the Populuxe era, the chief formal influence on the reclining chair came from transportation. The models for the recliner were the seats on railroad parlor cars and long-distance coaches and the passenger seats on airplanes, which had to be well cushioned to absorb some of the bumpiness of the ride. They reclined to allow the passenger a chance to rest. By the early 1950s, this pattern had spread to at least some cars. The front seat of the Nash was capable of folding down, so that the entire interior of the car would become a bed. Many other models began to offer adjustable seats as an option.

Charles Eames's rosewood-and-leather lounge chair, introduced in 1956. The adjustable recliner, with its various settings and options, embodied aggressive, dynamic relaxation.

For the furniture industry, the reclining chair did not imply any kind of revolution. It could be manufactured with the same materials and framing as a conventional easy chair and could be offered in the same general range of quality and price. This already gave it an edge over the Eames lounge, whose manufacture was non-standard and whose materials and detailing had to be of high quality because they were exposed. Still more important, however, the recliner was well suited to Populuxe marketing. With slight variations in design, the recliner could be sold as traditional or contemporary. It could be covered in vinyl or colonial fabrics or even real leather. It was well suited to receive changes or have special features.

Recliners that just sat on the floor could be supplanted by models that were platform rockers in their upright position. There could be intermediate positions, to allow the sitter to be laid back yet still sufficiently upright to watch television. And in its ultimate refinement, the chair could be outfitted with an electric motor to produce rapid vibration and what was called a "relaxing massage." This feature necessitated a control panel, which opened new possibilities for dials, variations in adjustment and other features that suggested technological progress. Such a chair could be more than just a chair, it could be therapy. It could be seen as a reward for undergoing the tensions and strains of daily life. And although it was likely to be bulky, with rounded rather than the angular lines most characteristic of the time, it used up-to-date thinking to foster an informal, comfortable way of living.

The recliner offered something else that was apparently very important to the Populuxe consumer. It *did* something. It did not just sit there. Service and convenience were the new watchwords of the era that produced the spray-steam-and-dry iron and the electric can opener. The Populuxe era was not a very good time for the furniture industry in general, as its share of the consumers' dollars declined steadily. There were, of course, more dollars to go around, and the trend toward homeownership and larger houses benefited the furniture industry. A lot of sofas, beds and cedar chests were sold. Dinettes boomed. But the trade press was filled with articles about how furniture manufacturers were losing out to such "competitors" as television, household appliances and automobiles. They agonized about how you can't go anywhere in a sofa, although one manufacturer of recliners featured an advertising campaign that suggested that the chair would transport you to a tropical paradise. Television and appliances were surely competition for furniture manufacturers because their promise was to make the home more pleasant and livable. But people became attached to their own familiar furniture far more strongly than they did to their toaster or electric mixer, and even in the late 1950s, at the height of the consumption frenzy, people typically kept each piece of living-room furniture for at least twelve years. Turnover was fastest in the kitchen, the room whose image was changing rapidly. Features were all. The steam iron with eight holes seemed clearly better than one with only four, and when that was supplanted by one with fifteen, you might think of buying a new one, especially since its holes ran the entire length of the iron instead of being clustered

Even the unmistakably rustic could have an air of modernity.

in the front. Most furniture simply did not have those apparently objective improvements in the service offered. It is hard to believe an iron could have more allure than a love seat, but in a sense it did. (Steam irons are cheaper than love seats, of course, but automobiles, which were sold largely on the basis of style, are a lot more expensive.)

Furniture manufacturers agonized over how to successfully make their previous products seem obsolete. There was the stereophonic easy chair, a 1957 invention that placed a speaker in each wing, but this sedentary predecessor to the Walkman never caught on. The furniture makers closely followed the *House & Garden* and *House Beautiful* color charts, but that was not enough. One argument held that if furniture makers would simply stop making the imitation Chippendale and Hepplewhite pieces and concentrate on doing modern designs, the industry would be better off. But those who believed that modernism was not a style but the appropriate response to twentieth-century life would not have liked the rest of the argument. The reason consumers should be weaned from historic periods was that modern would soon go out of style and something else would take its place. Furniture buyers would be as much slaves to fashion as automobile buyers and would be embarrassed not to purchase the latest model.

As things turned out, the next high style to come after modernism was post-modernism, which featured a return to the styles of the past. Thus, the strategy of force-feeding modernism wouldn't have worked, even had the large number of furniture manufacturers in America been able to agree to such a conspiracy. Indeed, purchasers of eclectic furniture, who were always in the majority, might be said to be post-modernists before their time. And like today's post-modernist architecture and furniture, most of what people bought during

Con-Tact paper turned anything into something else entirely.

Far left: All these draperies were modern, regardless of the style, because they were made of fiberglass and didn't need ironing. Left: With Applikay, a mid-fifties phenomenon, it was possible to get lively two-tones. Here, radiant pink is being applied in a silken fleece design on a Ramona green wall, while in the background, crystal green, in a falling feather pattern, covers caprice yellow.

the Populuxe era sought to be an evocation of the earlier style, not a duplicate of it. The manufacturers and writers for the decorating magazines underlined that point by saying that the splendor of the past had been adapted for modern living. And consumers didn't expect that their couch would be built by a craftsman, any more than they expected it of their Chevrolet. Drexel's factory in Virginia was turning out one complete bedroom set every minute. And to the rhetorical question of whether they would live in the world of Buck Rogers or that of Duncan Phyfe, the American consumer answered: both. This dismayed both the aesthetic reformers and the furniture manufacturers, both of whom were trying to get Americans to throw away their furniture, albeit for different reasons.

In any event, modernism, with its essentially ascetic attitudes, had little appeal to the emotions. Modernism consisted primarily of getting rid of things, of simplifying and clarifying. This idea won almost total acceptance in corporate architecture, in public buildings, in city planning and among intellectuals. Even in the home, the decorative excess of Victorianism was totally disapproved, and elegant simplicity was posited as the goal. But in the personal environment, clarity and simplicity were mitigated by the idea of enrichment, with Louis Sullivan and Frank Lloyd Wright cited as its forebears. Ornament was allowed, but with a pragmatic attitude. The goal was to "warm up" the modern materials and shapes with textures and patterns that made them less machinelike. While modernism was standardized and associated with the idea of social equality, enrichment was personal and associated with freedom of expression and of opportunity. The decorating magazines liked enrichment because it allowed them to promote a wide variety of products. It is a doctrine better suited to a consumer society, particularly one with newfound wealth.

For a significant upper-middle-class part of the market, Danish modern furniture provided the best of both worlds. It had light modern lines, carried out most often in teak, a luxurious tropical wood. The furniture that had the widest distribution and influence in this country represented only a small part of the spectrum of the design that was going on in Scandinavia, or even Denmark, at the time. The sculptural pieces by Arne Jacobsen, which were analogous in many ways to the work of Saarinen and Eames in this country, were less popular than the work of designers such as Hans Wegner, who stayed much closer to traditional styles. Wegner's ash-and-teak "peacock" chair, for example, had simple, graceful lines, but you didn't have to be an antiques expert to recognize it as a reworking of that American standard, the Windsor chair. If the Shakers had made sofas, they would probably have had something in common with one that Borge Mogenson made, which was detailed with thin leather laces. Danish modern allowed its buyers to feel that they were modern and respectful of the achievements of their own time and were purchasing honest, well-made furniture. At the same time, it had many of the virtues that their counterparts a few rungs down the professional and educational ladder were finding in adaptations of Early American. Danish modern, at its best, justified the decorating magazines' rhetoric of combining the best of old and new, looking both to tradition and to the future.

The Danish look had a great impact on domestic production too, because it inspired manufacturers to feature the wooden frame by exposing it and using loose foam cushions. They could have seen this idea in native mission-style furniture, but the inspiration for its 1950s manifestation came from Denmark.

While Danish modern brought visual enrichment through its use of natural materials, synthetics were embraced with enthusiasm. One of the most important was plastic laminate, of which Formica was the best-known brand. This material, which is still very much with us today, opened up new possibilities of color and pattern for all sorts of surfaces. It drove the enameled metal kitchen table out of business and became an integral part of the dinette. Because it was easier to keep clean, it allowed brighter colors on tables and counter tops, which had previously been covered with linoleum that was intended to hide the dirt. And Formica also invaded the living room. It replaced real wood on the tops of coffee tables and dining tables, preventing rings from the bottoms of glasses and worry over spills. It enabled furniture to stand up to a lot of abuse and thus carried out the goal of more relaxed and informal living. It didn't really look a whole lot like wood, but for many, the loss of the appearance of the real wood was a small price to pay for the convenience of a washable stain-resistant surface, even in the living room.

Some of what was done in the name of enrichment would have been depressing to Sullivan and surely was to Wright, although post-modernist theorists have found some of it enthralling. If you believe, for example, that beauty really is skin deep, you have to appreciate Con-Tact paper, a 1954 invention which resulted in an explosion of pattern all over the house. An adhesive-backed vinyl film, it would make almost any surface look something like marble, or stone, or bricks with ivy growing over them. There were bold stripes and squares in all the latest decorator colors. It could be wiped off with a cloth, and when it got worn, or even just a bit too familiar, it could be torn off and something else could be substituted. Con-Tact paper is almost pure symbol, something that serves as a reminder of something else but really doesn't look very much like it. It provided such an easy path to enrichment and change that it sometimes proved addictive.

Scandinavian-inspired furniture separated the wooden structure of chairs and sofas from the seats, which were foam cushions, and brought to modern furniture some of the qualities of early American.

The New Shape of Motion

One day during World War II, Harley Earl, the former Hollywood car customizer who, as head of the Art and Color section of General Motors, virtually invented automotive styling, got a distant look at something that inspired him. It was an airplane, the Lockheed P-38 Lightning. Earl had to stand thirty feet away, because this twin-engined fighter was still under security wraps. But this quick glimpse so excited Earl that it spurred him to create something that would help shape American culture for much of the next two decades. Earl beheld the P-38 and conceived the tailfin.

At least, this was the way Earl remembered it in 1953, after the tailfin had become a marked success on the Cadillac but before it appeared on virtually every car in America. The P-38-inspired tailfin was first seen on the 1948 Cadillac and encountered quite a lot of consumer resistance before it became wildly popular. As Earl put it, "It gave them an extra receipt for their money in the form of visible prestige marking for an expensive car." Unlike luxurious European cars, the Cadillac made little pretense of being handcrafted rather than mass-produced. It derived its luxurious identity from having something additional, a badge to attest that money has been spent. This is the function of the tailfin. Earl added that he liked the fins because they provided "graceful bulk," something he believed was characteristic of the American taste, and was certainly characteristic of his own.

By the time Earl told the story of the birth of the fin, he had been in the business of reshaping cars for more than thirty years. He did not come from an engineering background. Emotion, not machinery, was his starting point, and although he had to be concerned about production, his interest was not in making the cars but in selling them. Engineers might look for the perfect machine, while Earl and others who got into the styling business were trying to figure out the next dream. General Motors was the first to get into styling in a big way. It invented the annual model change, and its ability to get people excited about what was coming next helped bring it to its dominant position in the industry.

But although styling had been important before, by the mid-1950s, as *Collier's* put it, styling was "practically everything." Engineering, which had been a tremendous concern of automobile buyers in earlier times, had little appeal. Its only vestige was the horsepower rating—the bigger, the better. This preoccupation with styling seems to have grown out of public confidence in the quality of American automobiles. Many magazine and newspaper articles quoted people who said they thought all the cars were well made and they were all about the same. They felt the major choice they had was to find the car that made them feel good. This attitude lasted well into the 1960s, long after the introduction of the Corvair, the misdesigned car that was ultimately to shatter American confidence in Detroit's products.

Moreover, the automakers were well aware of the disappearance of the seller's market for automobiles which had begun immediately after the war and continued, according to one account, until the first week of August 1953. Some important things started to happen at that point. The overall number of cars sold stopped increasing. Chrysler Corporation, whose cars were the most conservatively designed, suffered sharply reduced sales, while Chevrolet held steady, and Ford, which had the raciest 1953 and 1954 designs, picked up about as many new buyers as Chrysler lost. The great expansion of the auto market was over, as nearly everyone who needed one had one. The automakers were faced with the challenge of selling automobiles to people who didn't really need them. Thus, they depended on styling to make people desire the car. "If we can bring out a new car that is a fine means of transportation, but makes you enthusiastic about going into the showroom to buy it, then we've done an excellent job," said William M. Schmidt, a Chrysler Corporation stylist. "We're really merchandisers."

This translates into giving everybody a symbolic receipt for his purchase. The tailfin had been accepted as a mark of luxury. It was inevitable that it would move down the line to all the buyers, especially those toward the bottom, where most cars were sold.

There is some irony in the choice of the P-38 as prototype for a new look, for although it was a beautiful airplane, and an effective one, its design did not have any long-range influence on aircraft. The plane had, in effect, three fu-

The Lockheed P-38 Lightning was one of the great fighter planes of World War II. Its distinctive profile was the inspiration for postwar Cadillacs.

selages—the central, smaller one contained the pilot and the controls, and each of the two outlying ones carried an engine and a fuel tank and was terminated with a vertical tail. Twin booms held it all together. At a time when airplanes in general were becoming thinner and more projectilelike, this one had visual qualities that resembled those of a catamaran. And although the proportions were somewhat different, the early finned Cadillacs had a somewhat tripartite composition themselves, with the sides larger and more muscular than the center.

Some years later, Earl glimpsed another airplane, the Douglas F-4D Skyray, this time in a newspaper photo. He ripped it out and put it in his pocket. When, in a casual conversation, he was asked where his next designs would come from, he pulled the picture out of his pocket and said, "I have it right here." He said he had done it for dramatic effect, but later decided he was right. The Skyray was in the news in 1953 because it briefly held the world speed record. It was a delta-wing craft, and from above or below its outline recalled that of the manta ray and related fish, hence its name. From the side, however, it was sharp, indeed needle-nosed. From the front, all you saw were its thin body, spreading wings and two parabolic air intakes. The Skyray never had as demonstrable an effect on General Motors cars as did the P-38, but it contained most of the imagery that not only GM but the entire automotive industry would use for several years. Earl's rash prediction about the Skyray made a fine ending for his 1953 first-person story in *The Saturday Evening Post,* however, because it did give his readers something to look forward to. Earl, who coined the term "dynamic obsolescence," was in the business of embodying fantasies. A car inspired by the hottest plane in the sky would simply have to be terrific.

The 1948 Cadillac was the first car with fins.

Jets, like the Douglas F-4D Skyray (below left), had more angular lines, echoed in the 1966 Plymouth (top), the 1955 Chevrolet (center), and the high-flying 1958 Buick (below).

By the time the article appeared, it had been determined that the tailfin would go democratic. Earl, whose styling operation had to work three years in advance of the production of a car, had already overseen much of the design of the 1955 Chevrolet. With this car, General Motors was attempting to confront the end of the seller's market and the decline in the number of potential buyers by giving its bread-and-butter product some excitement. The 1955 Chevy had tailfins, modest ones compared to those that would come just a few years later, but still tailfins. Their arrival on a Chevrolet expressed something very important about the time—the awareness that even the mass-market buyers of the bottom-of-the-line car had enough money to buy more than the basics. If the postwar Cadillac tailfin was the mark of the nouveau riche, the 1955 Chevrolet tailfin affirmed that nearly everyone was able to move up to luxury.

Moreover, as Earl's decision to change planes suggests, the 1955 Chevrolet tailfin was more up-to-date than anything that had yet appeared on a Cadillac because it was based on a more up-to-date airplane. Like the 1950 Fords and Studebakers, whose grilles suggested propellers, the Cadillacs' fins were developments of imagery from World War II. The 1955 Chevy was a jet-age car. Like several other new models unveiled in 1955, it had a new angular profile that was suggested by the latest airplanes.

It was the first stage of the transformation of cars to conform with what Chrysler Corporation advertising would later term "the new shape of motion." This referred to a new visual vocabulary, inspired by the jet and the rocket, that would manifest itself not only in automobiles but in home appliances, lampshades, fabric patterns, roadside architecture and almost everything else.

Despite rocket imagery, the 1953 Olds still had an old-fashioned rounded shape.

The streamlined shapes developed for earlier airplanes and trains and ocean liners had pervaded art and commerce for two decades. Suddenly, in the early 1950s, the geometry of straight lines and quarter circles began to seem downright antique. Streamlining had always been more a visual phenomenon than one based on scientific application, but the expression of aerodynamic qualities seemed appropriate to cars and trains in which a rounded streamlining could make a difference. In the early 1950s, jet-propelled airplanes so captured the imagination that the urge to look fast like a train was almost laughable. Automobiles were no longer really fast—by jet plane standards—so they strove to provide a visual echo of things that really moved fast. Cars like the early 1950s Nash, Hudson and Mercury, whose fully rounded shapes had only yesterday looked fast and thoroughly modern, began to evoke comparisons with tortoises and inverted bathtubs. And while such features as tailfins were retained, and even increased their expressive power, they too had to change. When they reached the masses, they had taken on a far more angular shape than their Cadillac and P-38 prototypes. The shape of the times had changed.

The airplanes of World War II had, for the most part, the classic rounded, streamlined look. Earl's exemplar, the P-38, was unusual in its appearance, but as with other airplanes of its time, its wings were at right angles to the fuselage. But even by the time the first tailfinned Cadillac was on the road, the most advanced aircraft design had been radically transformed by the capabilities of the jet engine and the physics of high-speed flight. During the late 1940s, during attempts to approach and break the sound barrier, it was determined that airplanes could go faster and encounter less wind resistance if their wings were swept back obliquely from the fuselage rather than being at the standard perpendicular. There was a loss of stability in the takeoff, however, and delta wings, in the shape of short triangles, were an attempt to solve that problem while enabling planes to go as fast as possible.

Thus the arrival of the acute angle as the most easily noticeable attribute of high-speed aircraft gave birth to a whole new visual vocabulary. The ideal of dynamism and modernity that had been expressed in streamlining remained constant, but the means of expressing it were transformed. Moreover, there was a sense that just as airplanes had broken through a barrier some had thought unbreakable, and were evaluated in terms that only shortly before had been unimaginable, modern life had broken through a barrier of its own and change and progress could be expected at a far more rapid rate than before.

The swept wing and delta wing gave airplanes a new look of forward thrust, indeed a dartlike quality, that had been missing in earlier airplanes. At the same time, the body of the airplane changed its shape. With the arrival of jets, the fuselage became a far more sculptural object. Almost all of its metal skin was curved in several directions. In profile, the plane appeared as a series of quite gentle curves that met at sharp points, the most dramatic of which was the nose. Where air intakes and other elements were attached to the side, the connection often took the form of a parabola, which itself became an abstraction of speed.

The fighter plane was what people thought of when they imagined a jet. It was the almost inevitable model for the automobile industry because it was the most romantic and also the most masculine and aggressive airplane. It was built for the highest speed and the greatest maneuverability. It was beginning to routinely break the sound barrier, and it was made to have a single pilot. Automobile fantasies tend to be personal, not social. A fighter pilot goes it alone. The Walter Mitty dream was updated to include a bubble-topped cockpit, and the *pocketa-pocketa* of the engine had given way to the mighty roar of the jet.

The Boeing 707 passenger jet was coming onto the scene at this time, and it was to have an important effect on personal travel habits and lead people to redefine their concepts of distance. But its speed was slow and its lines were boring compared to those of fighter planes and experimental aircraft. Indeed, Boeing hired the industrial designer-stylist Walter Dorwin Teague to make a design for the outside of the plane at the time it was being promoted and sold. His brown-and-gold scheme featured a number of jagged lines and gentle curves meeting at acute angles to make the pioneer passenger jet look a bit more like the jet of people's dreams.

Most aspects of jet aircraft design were about as applicable to an automobile as streamlining was to a stove. And those were the ones that proved influential. Unibody design, in which the entire body and framework were conceived as manufactured as a single unit, thus decreasing the weight and increasing the strength of the whole, was developed by the aircraft industry and adopted by auto manufacturers in Europe. But American manufacturers did not use the technology, because they were still organizing their manufacturing so that bodies were the result of one production process and chassis were part of another. Each had its own bureaucracy that was threatened by change. At the same time that the automobile companies were evoking the excitement of the jet age, they were organizing their plants to produce horseless carriages. The influence of aircraft technology was almost exclusively skin deep.

In 1954, General Motors unveiled something called the Firebird, an experimental show car meant for display in the very popular "Motoramas" the company held periodically in various American cities. These were exercises in marketing, not technology, and the cars shown were often simply versions of current models with heightened symbolic content, or trials of features that were a year or two away. Later, General Motors produced a car called the Firebird, but the Firebird of 1954 was never meant for the road. It was a literal translation of the fighter plane into what may have been an automobile. If it weren't for the four large, garishly hubcapped wheels, you would never guess it was an automobile. For one thing, it had wings, delta wings sticking out from the sides of the car and looking large enough to carry a real airplane, as long as there was a jet engine. In fact, it actually had a form of jet engine. The Firebird had a clear bubble top and a black-painted pointed nose and a single fin at the back. Earl himself designed this Firebird, and two subsequent ones

General Motors's experimental Firebird of 1954 carried airplane imagery as far as it could go, without taking off.

that were a bit less fantastic. Firebird 2 had many titanium components, just like a real jet. Earl said at the time that the construction of the prototype brought titanium production cars fifteen years closer. We're still waiting. The Firebirds were obviously never intended as prototypes for cars that might someday be produced. Rather they were affirmations of an aspiration toward limitless power, lightning speed and the desire of Americans, as individuals, to participate in the technological revolution that was happening all around them.

It was a long way down from that visionary needle-nosed, one-seater Firebird to the Chevrolet, which had long had the reputation of being good basic transportation, the car for little old ladies who used it only for church on Sunday and for others who craved dependability and did not expect much psychic satisfaction. In 1955, however, all that changed. The dull little car, which had been available in colors like dark blue, dark green and deep violet, all of which seemed only to be gradations of basic black, came forth in color combinations like coral and charcoal gray. It had real tailfins, jagged chrome accents and lines that were sharp and modern. It was over-powered by Chevrolet's first V-8 engine. There were even widespread rumors that under certain conditions it would fly off the ground. The week of its unveiling, which was budgeted at $3.5 million and was one of the most extensive media events ever, advertisements in popular magazines showed it not on a road but on a runway, next to a jet fighter. Some 20 million people came to the various unveiling events around the country.

A station wagon for Mom and a T-Bird for Dad was what Dad, at least, aspired to.

And Chevrolet was not alone. All of Chrysler Corporation's models, including the low-priced Plymouth, were restyled that year, with the unveiling of the "Forward Look," signaling its adoption of the pointed tailfin and other jet-age accouterments. Ford, whose styling had been livelier than either of its low-priced rivals, had only the merest suggestion of tailfins, but its lines dramatized length and dynamism. The result was an automobile-buying frenzy. By the end of 1955, Americans had spent $65 billion on automobiles, an amount equal to 20 percent of the gross national product. That year, General Motors became the first company to earn $1 billion in a single year, and it produced its 50 millionth car. It was a Chevrolet that was sprayed with gold paint and finished with 24-karat-gold-plated screws and body trim and shown around the country. It was not the solid-gold Cadillac but its cousin, the gold-plated Chevy, that provided the emblem of its time.

The 1955 models marked a turning point in American automotive design and the triumph of Populuxe in the marketplace. The ever-greater elaboration of jet-age styling meant that it was not only the Cadillac buyer but everyman who would pay extra to get that additional, non-functional mark of luxury. Indeed, the automakers seemed to have confounded predictions of the collapse of the automobile market. They had not only sold more car per car, they had actually sold more cars, period. Throughout the rest of the decade, the automakers would strive to sell ever more car to each buyer, and the phrase "a lot of car for the money" became a standard part of the salesman's pitch. Chevrolet, Ford and Plymouth had changed seemingly overnight from conservative family cars to high-powered and fast-looking machines. That woke up a lot of buyers and spurred them to make a purchase, but it left the carmakers with the dilemma of what to do for an encore.

There were other big changes in America that had set the stage for the auto-mad 1955 model year and the blossoming of the Populuxe approach to automobile styling. The most important was the continuing transformation of the American landscape and the emergence of the new, automobile-dependent suburbia as the dominant market. In that environment, one car was essential, two cars were almost essential. The automobile ceased to be symbolic of the family as a whole and became, instead, the possession of the person who usually drove it. That opened new possibilities for color and styling and highly profitable optional features. Each buyer was offered such a range of choices that the manufacturers were able to pretend that each car was a special expression of the taste and attitude of the person who drove it. Gone was the dignity and stability of the family car, which required an almost institutional expression. It was replaced by a quest for self-realization, which encouraged quirky and perverse expressions of personality. Even station wagons lost their dowdy crate-on-wheels quality and became stylish and dynamic. In 1955, the Chevy Nomad wagon was cited along with the Ford Thunderbird, which was also introduced that model year, as the most beautiful new car. Indeed, the combination of Nomad for Mom and T-bird for Dad was close to the ideal.

The Thunderbird took even its creators by surprise. Despite the similarity in name, it had little in common with Earl's futuristic Firebird. It lacked futuristic imagery. It was short when everything else was getting longer. And it was possible to purchase one, although sometimes delivery might take a while. It was, in fact, the prototypical personal car, but when it appeared the industry seemed not to grasp its significance. It was a two-seater at the outset, which meant that it went completely against the grain of a family-centered society. Yet there it was, reaching a much larger market than anyone had predicted. It was a dream of irresponsibility, detachment, escape that could appeal only to a small minority of the market. But it expressed some very potent desires which Ford was able to deliver in more compromised form in its other models. And in 1958, when a token back seat was added, car buffs howled, but sales shot up. The design had lost much of its brashness and charm, but clearly more people could justify this very personal indulgence if they could be assured they could drive the kids somewhere in an emergency. The four-seater Thunderbird carried the promise that it was possible to have it all. During the recession year of 1958, when almost all cars took big losses, only two models did very well—the compact Rambler and the somewhat compact but very flashy and expensive Thunderbird.

That was also the year of one of the most famous debacles in the history of the automobile industry—the Edsel. Perhaps the most prepared-for automobile in history, it was the result of years of marketing studies which showed that there was a demand for a car for the young executive. The poet Marianne Moore was hired to come up with a name. She suggested Silver Sword and Resilient Bullet, the Ford Fabergé and the Pastelogram. She also tried the Anticipator and the Mongoose Civique. Her final try produced the Utopian Turtletop, but by that time she was probably just having fun. Naming it for Henry Ford II's father wasn't her idea. Her endeavor came to an end when she got a letter saying it would be called Edsel. "I know you will share your sympathies with us," the letter concluded.

When the car finally came out, the market was extremely unsympathetic. Edsel sounded like a funny word, and its styling, though not far outside the mainstream of its time, was widely criticized. Its most distinctive feature was a front end with a vertical central grille, which prompted the wisecrack that it looked like an Oldsmobile sucking a lemon. Others found the grille to be rather like a vagina. At any rate, people were laughing at the grille from the moment it came out. Its fins emerged from concave panels at the rear end, a motif that was also used by the Chevrolet, the Buick and several other cars that year. But it was a short-lived look that proved unpopular with the public. So many Edsels were given away in contests that those few people who actually bought one had to put up with wise guys asking, "Where did you win yours?" Edsel suffered from bad timing, coming out as it did during a recession, and it was hardly one of the most beautiful cars in history. But its biggest mistake was its assumption that the young executive on his way up would want a glittering, opulent family boat. What the young executive really wanted was another Ford product, the Thunderbird, and Ford wasn't able to make enough of them.

The high Populuxe era of automobile styling is one from which many design historians choose to avert their gaze, as if from a particularly gruesome highway accident. It was, they say, an unfortunate setback in what had generally been a period of progress in automotive design. The image of the horseless carriage lingered for decades after the invention of the automobile, and only during the 1930s was the car widely conceived as a unified form with a shape and nature of its own. The 1940s were largely lost to World War II, but the progress of the 1930s was continued in the early 1950s. Then, suddenly, cars started trying to be airplanes. Good sense had given way to the demands of marketing and trim conquered the car.

In 1955, the year of the big change, the pioneer industrial designer Raymond Loewy, whose long-term consultant relationship with Studebaker had just broken off, condemned the new models in a speech to the Society of Automobile Engineers, later reprinted in *The Atlantic Monthly*. He called the typical new car a "jukebox on wheels." "Is it responsible," he asked, "to camouflage one of America's most remarkable machines as a piece of gaudy merchandise? . . . Form, which should be the cleancut expression of mechanical excellence, has become sensuous and organic." The intervening decades have weakened those two adjectives as terms of condemnation, but he focused on a key issue. The automobile is not a living thing; it is a machine. But often people don't care to think of it in that way.

Surely today, such relatively plain and honest cars as the Fords of 1949–52, and especially the Studebakers designed under Loewy's supervision during the late 1940s and early 1950s, look better than what came after. The 1953 Studebaker coupes do not seem a bit dated. They speak as vividly of the romance of the automobile and moving at great speed as any car of the decade, but they do so cleanly and practically. What makes them so exciting today is that they were conceived entirely as automobiles, without making any analogies to any other form. At the time, though, they really did look funny. For more than five years, "Which way is it going?" was considered a witty question to ask a Studebaker driver.

When the nearly faceless Studebakers came out in 1953, however, they were still way ahead of their time. If Harley Earl had put General Motors behind a design like the 1953 Studebakers, it might have worked. It took some time for tailfins to catch on, after all. Studebaker, an independent, lacked GM's power to set the new styles simply by manufacturing them. And although Loewy himself did much to develop and propagate the idea that the way people feel about a machine is an essential ingredient in the way it will eventually work, Earl, with his dogmas of leonine fronts and graceful bulk, worked at a level of emotion and metaphor Loewy never touched. Earl understood that people sometimes buy new cars to become a new sort of person. In 1953, the year Loewy won critical adulation and disappointing sales for his coupes, Earl and GM introduced bullet-shaped protuberances above the front bumpers of several Cadillac models. These non-functional, expensive-to-repair pieces of

chrome were known in the business as "bombs," or more commonly "Dagmars," in honor of an extremely busty, none-too-bright blond bombshell of late-night television. It was perhaps quixotic for Loewy and Studebaker to make a lean, pure automobile in the same year that General Motors was developing breasts. And, of course, the breasts sold. Cadillacs had Dagmars for a decade, and several other automobile makes adopted them as well. They were laughed at, but they raised sales.

The new always has a problem in winning public acceptance, and those classic Studebakers had very little time. The yearly model change was institutionalized by GM chairman Alfred P. Sloan, and praised in 1955 by GM president Harlow Curtice as "the most important single factor responsible for the growth and vitality of [the automobile] industry." It promised, in effect, that each year cars would be better than the year before. Retooling costs often ran in the hundreds of millions of non-inflated dollars. Studebaker did not have the economies of scale that GM had, and could not make major changes every year, but neither could it afford to wait for years for the public to discover it was selling a classic car. The car had to change, and Studebaker just kept adding more trim and generally messing up the superb design, which did not help sales at all.

Perhaps nothing could have. Studebaker kept selling its cars on the basis of innovative car design while General Motors stayed securely with analogy. It was easier, somehow, to understand a car that looked like a chorus girl coming and a fighter plane going than it was to make sense of a car that was just trying to be better at looking like a car.

Earl himself was never after the perfect design, just many different ones that would appeal to various fantasies at various price levels. Because most people did not understand the fine points of the engineering of their cars, and because improvements in engineering were made less often than GM wanted the public to believe, Earl's contribution was to give form, indeed many different forms, to the annual model change. Loewy's work for Studebaker was intended to shake up the industry and create a product to beef up that independent automaker's share of the market. Earl's work at GM was dedicated to change for its own sake. His philosophy of dynamic obsolescence generally implied carefully calibrated change. If he were to set a course toward, say, larger rear windows, it would rarely happen all at once. Thus, each year's model would have a little bit more glass and hence appear a little bit newer. Rather than produce an ideal design and then junk it up in the name of novelty, GM would produce a target design and move gradually toward it, until the target was once again changed.

Most cars of the Populuxe era were profoundly mixed metaphors. They strove to express attributes that were inherently contradictory. They became ever longer, ever lower in the effort to look fast and dynamic. "My sense of proportion tells me that oblongs are more attractive than squares," Earl wrote, "just as a ranch house is more attractive than a square, three-story flat-roofed house or a greyhound is more attractive than a bulldog." Yet if you look at the grilles of the cars produced at General Motors during Earl's tenure, you see

heavy chrome, major sculptural elements and an overall feel of aggressiveness. They may have been greyhounds from the side, but very often they were bull-dogs from the front. Also contradicting the desire to look sleek and fleet was the need to look sufficiently weighty. Increasingly, every car was being sold as a variation of a luxury car, and the one thing Americans knew about the luxurious was that it should be big, soft and heavy. In 1955, the average American car went twenty miles on a gallon of gas, a feat that has been equaled only recently. At the same time that cars were starting to take off into the jet age, they began to gain quite a lot of weight.

The images evoked by automobiles vary, depending on which part of the car you examine. Surely, the front of a car is facelike, which is why automobile designers routinely referred to the radiator as the mouth and chrome uprights in the radiators as teeth. Throughout the early 1950s, the faces of cars tended toward hostility and defensiveness, especially on the big cars, but also on Chevrolets and Plymouths. The chrome was thick. The teeth were large, the bumpers suggested armor. One is tempted to find the countenance of Senator Joseph McCarthy glaring out defensively from their front ends. The pugnacious grilles provided a mobile image of an America obsessed with finding and fighting enemies within.

That image changed in the Populuxe era. Cars gained a friendlier look. If they had teeth they were smaller, but the mouth often stretched the entire width of the car in an almost Eisenhowerish smile. Headlights developed rather large and protruding eyebrows, but these did not project a defensive air as much as an urge to move forward. A few cars, notably the late 1950s Dodges, maintained a fierce, toothy image with catlike eyes, but they were peaceful compared to what had been on the road earlier in the decade. Pontiacs split their grilles and lost their facial imagery almost completely, but they had bumpers with the heft and shape of battering rams. Overall, the lightening up of the front end was a significant change in automobile styling, and it was used as the occasion for a lot of advertising that celebrated elegant simplicity, even as other parts of the cars became more and more elaborate.

As cars became steadily lower, and especially when dual headlights arrived in 1957 and 1958, the facelike quality was suppressed as the eyes and mouth tended to merge into a single horizontal combination. This look took hold in the early 1960s, obliterating Earl's leonine imagery and replacing it with an aspect that was decidedly fishlike. That's when cars started to get names like Marlin and Barracuda. Earl had long been fascinated with the dorsal fin of a shark, and he had dream cars made with a single fin, placed in the center of the rear end, right where it would block visibility to the rear. That's probably why one was never manufactured, but fish imagery on cars is still with us, and almost inevitably, Earl was there first.

With the invention of the tailfin, Earl had moved the focus of attention in automobiles from the front of the car to the rear and begun the tailfin explosion which would reach its peak in 1959 and gradually recede during the 1960s. From the moment they became widespread, their demise was predicted, on

the grounds that there are only so many things that can be done with fins. This proved to be true, but not before automobiles had sprouted even more variations than anyone could possibly have predicted.

Earl's first fins were taken from the twin tails of the P-38, where they were mounted vertically and intended to stabilize the airplane. Cadillac fins, although they became sharper during the Populuxe era, stayed with the image of stability. So did the various Chrysler models, on which the fins were even advertised, a bit dishonestly, as providing "stability at speed," another ideal of the period. Up until 1956, tailfins invariably contained taillights, either in the more streamlined Cadillac style or cut back at an angle as they were on Chevrolets and Plymouths. On Fords, the fins were little more than vertical accents to the cylinder shape generated by its characteristic round taillights.

But on many models after 1957, the fin was set free of the taillight, which either became an almost incidental part of the fin or was placed somewhere else entirely. On some Cadillacs and a few other cars, the taillights broke free of the body and took on a form that recalled that of a small jet engine. Meanwhile the fin went even higher and took on blade shapes, slab shapes, extremely pointed shapes. In 1958, the composite fin emerged. On Dodges, for example, one fin appeared to grow out of the top of another. On the Mercury Turnpike Cruiser, two fins appeared to grow through each other, giving each fin an X-shaped profile. In some of the 1960 Chrysler products, shark fins appeared to be growing out of airplane-inspired fins.

At the same time, some cars deserted the illusion that fins were strong stabilizers at the sides of the car. Instead, the rear panels of the car were concave, and the fins appeared to be gouged out of a solid mass. This was the look of the 1958 Chevrolet, Buick, Oldsmobile and Edsel. Most of these lacked the sense of dynamism of the best finned creations. But once the fins stopped being entirely vertical, they were allowed to spread out and become what they had always threatened to be—wings. The promise of the Firebird was at least partially fulfilled with the 1959 Chevrolet, one of the most outrageous cars of the period, whose enormous rear deck had a bat-wing shape that resulted in, among other things, a V-shaped trunk lid. People joked that the rear end was long enough to land an airplane on, but the car really looked as if it were going to take off itself. That same year the square, more T-bird-like Ford with just the hint of wings sold more cars than Chevy. But in the next year, 1960, the Ford sprouted larger wings, and the Chevy's wings got more subdued and horizontal. The result was that the two cars looked very much alike, with their design converging from different directions.

"Take all the fins off," said Ford styling executive Robert H. Maguire, "and you have a piece of soap with wheels on it. Those fins finish off the metal. They give full length to the car." He said that late in 1958, when Ford fins were belatedly getting larger. But only a few years later, they were gone completely.

The other strong influence from aviation was the bubble-topped cockpit. A few cars actually offered optional clear tops, but it was quickly discovered that these baked the occupants of the car, or at least the upholstery. The compro-

mise was the wraparound windshield, which at least gave the illusion of un-restricted panoramic vision, even though it also caused a lot of people to hit their knees on the extra bit of framing that was required to support it whenever they got into or out of the car. It was less wonderful than it promised to be, because the curved glass caused distortion. By some estimates at the time, as much as a third of the glass surface was unusable. And in the rain it became much less, because there were no wraparound windshield wipers. The wrap-around windshield was introduced with great fanfare and customer enthusi-asm in 1953. During the mid-1950s, it was considered the very essence of modernity, but when it disappeared a decade later, nobody seemed to notice.

One can view the years from 1955 to 1960 as the great age of automobile styling. Despite criticism at the time that cars were copying from each other and starting to look alike, there was variety, color and nerve in automobile designs. Sometimes they went way too far, but that was one reason why people actually looked forward to seeing what the new cars would look like. They were changing faster than they ever had before, and in more and more extravagant ways. The era began in euphoria with the record 1955 model year, and reached its nadir in 1958 with the disastrous introduction of the Edsel and the near-collapse of the entire automobile market. Styling was credited with success, so it had to take a large part of the blame for downturns. Yet even in bad times, people bought the cars that were designed to look as big as possible, because they believed in getting more car for the money. Foreign imports were just starting to make some inroads, but one Ford executive probably spoke for the industry when he said that Volkswagens were bought not by those who needed economical transportation but by "gray-flannel nonconformists." Moreover, he was probably right.

But at the same time that it was a kind of golden age, the very profusion of designs, the unceasing novelty, provided an indication that the system was somehow breaking down. Cars had never before changed their shapes as rap-idly as they did during the Populuxe era. Most of the large companies had been in a cycle of major change every three years with face-lifts in between, but starting in 1955, many models got major changeovers every two years, and in a few cases, each year, and the face-lifts became more drastic too. The need to produce an array of cars which appeared to be totally new every year some-times led designers to great flights of imagination, but it also encouraged them to be arbitrary. Earlier, newness had appeared on the American car inch by inch. During the late 1950s, this gradualism disappeared as cars attempted to transform themselves and fill a larger place in people's consciousness, not to mention their garages. As *Business Week* said in 1959, planned obsolescence wasn't getting a chance to work.

Even at GM, the careful calibrations implicit in Earl's approach were aban-doned. In 1959, for example, the Buick, which had always been round, and a little bit bulky, with the distinctive character of a souped-up dowager, was to-tally made over. It turned angular and unrecognizable, with slanted dual head-lights, a front end that suggested wings and a back that had some. It even lost

The Edsel was one of the most carefully planned cars in history, and one of the biggest disasters. Derision focused on its vertical grille.

its trademark portholes. Thus a look that had been developed over three decades was totally discarded. It was not the wildest car of the year; there was plenty of competition. But it was the most shocking, because it broke completely with the strongest surviving tradition, one Earl had shaped from the start. The search for new looks bordered on the desperate, while fantasy, so carefully measured before, started to run wild.

The need for incessant novelty took its toll on the creative people in the industry. George Walker, Earl's counterpart at Ford, expressed the dilemma well in a 1959 interview: "The 1957 Ford was great, but right away we had to bury it and start another. We design a car, and the minute it's done, we hate it—we've got to do another one. We design a car to make a man unhappy with his 1957 Ford 'long about the end of 1958." Walker was boasting, but there seems to be a note of exasperation in his comments, which is understandable. There was a sense at the time that the whole process was careening out of control, even as the public was starting to become jaded.

The Ford Skyliner was truly a hardtop convertible. There were two problems: the trunk had to be completely empty to put the top down, and much of the time the top didn't go down no matter what you did.

The career of Virgil Exner, vice president and chief of styling for Chrysler Corporation from 1952 to 1962, illustrates the powers and perils of styling. While Earl had virtually invented styling, Exner was the key stylist of the Populuxe era. He oversaw the building of some of the most graceful cars of the time, and some of the most garish. During his career at Chrysler, he sought the expertise of the top European car builders, and in a speech early in his tenure, he took what many understood to be a swipe at Earl by denouncing "the ponderous, massive Hollywood concepts which have taken root in the field of automobile design." But a few years later, he brought Earl's invention, the tailfin, to its greatest height. Under Exner's direction, low-priced cars became larger and felt more luxurious than ever before. Then he suffered when buyers discovered that they weren't quite as good as they looked.

Exner had started out at General Motors under Earl during the 1930s, and he rapidly rose to head of styling at Pontiac, where he invented the kind of chrome trim that became known as speed whiskers. In 1939, he joined Loewy's office, where he was largely responsible for the design of the 1947 Studebaker Champion, one of the first markedly postwar cars, and one that, unlike the classic 1953, sold well.

For several years after he joined Chrysler in 1949, its management was hostile to styling, and most of its models followed what the industry called three-box design—two on the bottom and one on top. Chrysler ads stressed engineering and basic soundness, and by late 1953, sales of Plymouths, Dodges, De Sotos and Chryslers were plummeting. When Exner was called upon to supervise a total makeover of all Chrysler's models for 1955, it appeared to many as if the future of the company was on the line. He was, as *Look* put it, a "stylist on the spot." The designs, which inaugurated the "Forward Look," were radical compared with the previous year's models. They were longer and lower, they had "Frenched headlights," which meant that their eyebrows protruded, as if the front of the car was struggling to go ahead, even when it was parked. The boxiness was gone. Exner had said cars should look poised and eager, and these did. Even though they still had a lot of round, semi-streamlined features left, the headlights, taillights and two-toning introduced the new angular style. One trade magazine worried that the look would

Virgil Exner gave all of Chrysler Corporation's products the "Forward Look" in 1955, and they followed the shape, shown here in a 1958 advertisement, for the next five years.

prove too sophisticated for the American buyer, while another said the image sought to evoke "Marilyn Monroe as a housewife." For the writer to associate the distinctly rounded image of Monroe with the new angular features of the cars seems incongruous. But it does indicate the glamour of the angular look, the promise of excitement and escape from the domestic routine. The rounded look was familiar and comfortable; the angles seductive. Chrysler's "Forward Look" encompassed not only new car styles but a new corporate logo of two superimposed boomerang shapes, which had become the most popular graphic image of dynamism at the time.

In 1957, the slogan was "Suddenly it's 1960!" The cars were dramatically longer, and the tailfins soared up from the fenders to make the cars appear both more dynamic and more substantial than they had been before. The 1955 Chevrolet had brought a charge of excitement that changed the practical family car into a whole new animal; the 1957 Chrysler line promised a level of roominess and sheer pretentiousness that had previously been available only at the top of the line. Chrysler's corporate advertisements promised "the new shape of motion." Today, these cars seem to be about as good-looking as cars with tailfins ever got, and the public agreed by buying a lot of them. These cars had a graceful wedge-shaped profile that was inevitably compared to that of a fighter plane. The Dodge, in which the tailfin seemed to begin at the headlight and rise the entire length of the car, was probably the most handsome. The Plymouth, whose fins rose sharply to a plateau, was less elegant as a design, but it was unquestionably more vulgar, which was probably what the company had in mind. By this time, all the American automakers had tacitly acknowledged the Cadillac as the standard to which Americans aspired. Cadillac's advertising was aimed clearly at the nouveau riche, telling them that now that they'd made it they deserved a Cadillac. In 1957, *The New Yorker* ran a cartoon that showed a troubled man on a psychiatrist's couch complaining, "I'm 46, and I'm still driving one of the low-priced three." The 1957 Chrysler products were trying to put such minds at ease by demonstrating to consumers that while they were trying to make it, they needn't sacrifice too much. They could get Cadillac length and Cadillac showiness in a low-priced car that was all new in a year when most other brands were in the latter stages of recycling

The 1957 Plymouth was bigger than any of the "low-priced three" had ever been.

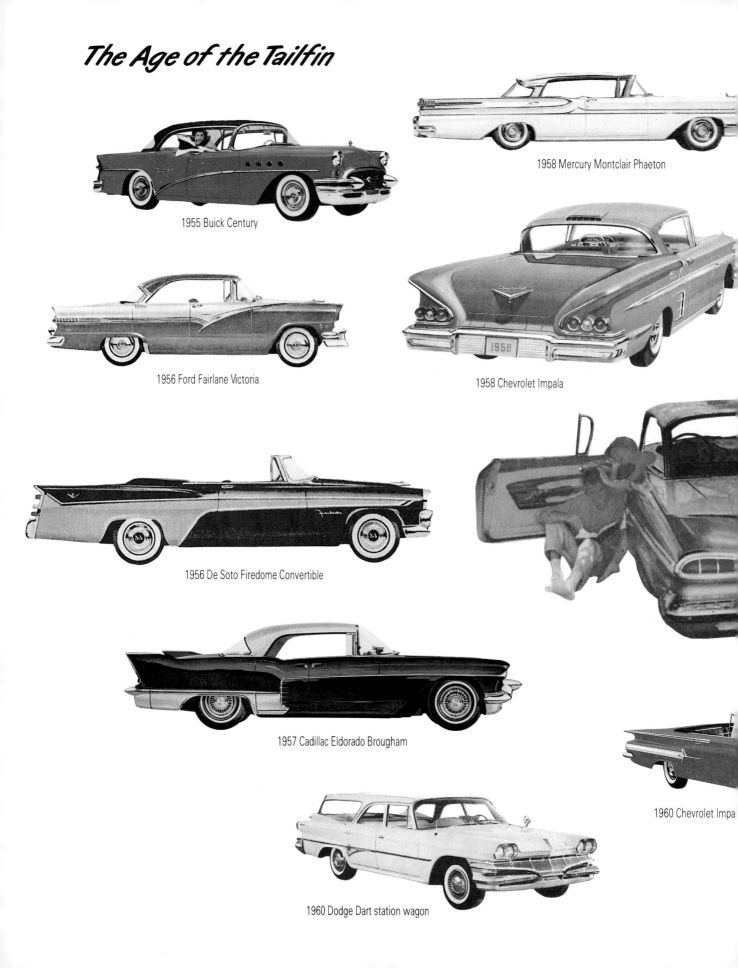

The Age of the Tailfin

1958 Mercury Montclair Phaeton

1955 Buick Century

1956 Ford Fairlane Victoria

1958 Chevrolet Impala

1956 De Soto Firedome Convertible

1957 Cadillac Eldorado Brougham

1960 Chevrolet Impa

1960 Dodge Dart station wagon

1960 Plymouth Fury

1962 Chrysler Newport

1960 Cadillac Fleetwood

1962 Chevrolet Impala

1959 Chevrolet Impala

1961 Ford Falcon

1960 Ford Thunderbird

1964 Cadillac Coupe de Ville

their 1955s. Another way of looking at it was that everyone who had the money to buy a Plymouth had indeed "made it." Such people didn't have to deny themselves anything.

In Detroit, these designs were hailed as "gasaroony," which *Popular Mechanics* translated as stylists' talk meaning "terrific, overpowering, weird." Those in the industry even found a measure of restraint in these designs, since they got nearly all their drama from form and line and did not depend on extraneous chrome and brightwork for their effect. There was even a concern that they were too tasteful and that a little bit of "gorp," as aggressive bumpers, dazzling hubcaps and other forms of automotive razzle-dazzle were termed, might make the cars more attractive to the public. Meanwhile, in New York and in Europe, Exner, designer of the admirable Studebaker and follower of Loewy, emerged as an apostate. He had led Chrysler, the last stronghold of engineering and sanity in the industry, away from substance and into flash.

The 1957s were restrained compared with what was to come during the next two years. While fins seemed to be trying to break free of the cars and ascend into the heavens, new chrome, protruding lights, mean-looking grilles and other pieces of stylists' spaghetti added burdens that kept them thoroughly earthbound. The 1958 models did not sell well, partly because of a national economic recession that gave all the automakers a disastrous year. But it was worsened for Chrysler because those long, luxurious 1957s had a tendency to rust. The beauty was skin deep, after all, and the skin was rotting away. In 1959, a full-scale tailfin backlash was underway, and Chrysler was out on the market with models that had tailfins on top of their tailfins. By the early 1960s, fins had gone about as far as they could go. Chrysler kept them, but the designers turned their attention to doing particularly ugly things to the cars' front ends to make them seem sharper. Concave forms, which had never been successful at the rear of cars, were even worse at the front. One Chrysler model even had its headlights on little stanchions, a return to the days of the horseless carriage. Its imagery, however, was not that of the horseless carriage but that of a low-budget Hollywood vision of little men from outer space, with eyes at the ends of little stalks, like a lobster's.

In 1960, each of the Big Three produced a compact model, essentially to give automobile buyers the chance to buy a car of the approximate size and simplicity of the standard pre-1955 automobile. Ford's Falcon, which proved to be the sales leader, was clearly a truncated Ford. Chevrolet's Corvair, the first

The 1959 Cadillac featured tailfins with pendulous, bomblike tail lights.

In 1962, the Wide-Track Pontiac pushed Plymouth out of third place in sales, and its advertising didn't even show the back of the car.

major model introduction in which Earl had no role, was a rear-engine car whose flat, symmetrical fore and aft styling revived those "can't tell if it's coming or going" Studebaker jokes. At Chrysler, the "good" Exner returned with the design of the compact Valiant, which was halfway between these two approaches. It had a vaguely European look with a badge-shaped grille and other elements taken from an Italian-produced "idea car" of many years before. The Valiant was the only compact with fins, but they were neatly tucked over the fenders. They looked more like a bird's wings than a jet's. Of the three compacts, the Valiant was the one that best balanced practicality with the fantasy people had come to expect in cars of any size.

The critical and commercial success of the Valiant may have been Exner's downfall. Chrysler's management decided in 1960 that the massive increase in size, weight and decoration that they had done so much to promote was about to run its course, and they began to reduce the size of all their models. The 1962 models started to undo what Chrysler had done in 1957. Although in most marketing surveys Americans said they wanted smaller and more sensible models, it was well established by that time that they almost always lie. (Ford had discovered it could get a more accurate idea of consumer preferences by asking people what they thought their neighbors would want to buy.) In 1959, Exner himself had said, "Stylists don't like a lot of chrome, but people have demanded it over the years. Every attempt that I know of to strip a car, to take off the chrome, has met with failure."

Chrysler's return to the sensible met with the same results. The 1960s proved to be the heyday of the American monster car, the kind that would roar down the interstate while pampering its occupants with "living-room comfort." The exemplary car of the 1960s was the Wide-Track Pontiac. It had a new kind of chassis, introduced in 1959, which put the wheels closer to the edge of the frame. Pontiac turned attention from the profile of the car to the front and rear, where it featured extremely aggressive bumpers, split-grille designs and large horizontal lights. After all these years in which cars boasted of being longer and lower, Pontiac bragged about being wider, and it worked. In 1962, Pontiac pushed Plymouth out of third place in sales, and it stayed there for the rest of the decade. The decision to go smaller pushed Chrysler back into the kind of crisis from which Exner's designs had done so much to rescue it a decade

before. Exner and other top managers were fired in 1962, and Chrysler recovered again, though it was never the styling leader it was in Exner's day.

Exner seems ultimately to have been overwhelmed by the demands of constantly producing stylistic novelty. It may even be true that Exner was the tasteful idealist many had thought him to be and he fell from grace while trying to do the right thing. Or he may merely have been eager to try something different. No matter, the big, showy late-1950s Chrysler products Exner developed truly set the shape of the American family car for the 1960s. They were also all too susceptible to the charge that they were "gas-guzzling dinosaurs," as the American Motors advertising called them.

But the American appetite for the dinosaurs had not disappeared. The early 1960s were a period not so much of extinction as of domestication. The cars became less flamboyant about their size and weight, because those two qualities were no longer new. Automobile companies increased their dependence on profitable options, in order to heighten the illusion that "we're building this car for you." Colors became less vibrant, and what two-toning remained became very low-key.

But the changes of the earlier years had been consolidated. Even poorer people, who bought used cars rather than new ones, had become used to larger cars. Even the compacts began that typical American cycle of growing larger and heavier and filling up with options and additional features. What was missing was the rampant vulgarity and joy of the Populuxe era, the sense that a new car is an achievement worth celebrating. All cars became squarer. It became more and more difficult to tell them apart. The vision of luxury that once had been dramatized with soaring fins no longer needed to be so strongly accented. What the mid-1950s had called superhighways were, by the early 1960s, the roads to work. And they were jammed with big, comfortable cars.

The Boomerang and Other Enthusiasms

When Raymond Loewy called the 1955 cars jukeboxes on wheels, he meant to condemn automobiles for becoming loud, colorful and vulgar, like the entertainment machines he believed embodied the worst of American culture. As it turned out, the influence of the late-1950s cars would end up transforming the jukebox. As the 1950s progressed, the familiar, flashing, curvy, arch-topped jukeboxes disappeared from bars and diners to be replaced by newer models that played 45 rpm records, the new standard for pop singles. These new jukeboxes had a lot more glass, wrapping all the way around the record storage and playing mechanism. But this new transparency did not appear to serve those who were dropping their coins into the slot and pressing the buttons. Rather, it seemed more as if the jukebox itself had turned into a vehicle of sorts, one that incorporated the kind of transparency that would be found in a jet plane or a new car. The whole machine had angular lines and tended to lean forward, poised and eager like an Exner-designed car.

The jukebox wasn't going anywhere, physically at least, but symbolically it was a harbinger of the new. It was delivering the latest music at a moment when the music was itself shaped by new stirrings of sensuality and dynamism. The heavy-looking old jukebox still had memories of Glenn Miller bouncing around inside. The new-style jukebox, which was both larger and airier-looking than the old one, matched the new Chevy V-8 as a symbol of teenage liberation and was the appropriate vessel for "Rock Around the Clock," "Peggy Sue" and "Hound Dog."

One other interesting thing happened to the jukebox during this period—it started to spin off satellites. Each diner, drive-in or tavern booth was equipped with a mini-jukebox of its own, complete with a flip-page list of selections under glass, its own coin slot and even its own speaker, two after stereo came in. No longer did people have to get up from their tables, walk across the room, check out the selections and put the money in the slot. Groups at the tables could decide what they were going to play together. Arguments over the selection could even replace conversation. The jukebox had become suburbanized, and the main jukebox, like the old downtowns, assumed a subordinate, symbolic function. The only people who had to go to the main jukebox were those who couldn't get a booth. That meant that the main jukebox no longer needed to have the color and hearthlike qualities of the old jukeboxes, but it did need to have the iconography of dynamism. This look was set more than anything else by cars, which were in turn trying to capture the dynamism of the jet plane and the rocket. And all had to harmonize with a new way of living that was increasingly suburban, increasingly mobile, physically fragmented but tuned to the same channel.

Then, as now, people were bombarded with imagery through advertising, television, magazines, movies, fine art, architecture, store design, industrial design. And while many of these images were competing with one another and attempting to pull people in different directions, there was also an overall coherence to these images. Orange-juice pitchers seemed somehow to rhyme with cars and jukeboxes. Images of stars, and of the points of the compass, and of chemical structure all merge into a look that is unmistakably of its time.

Dynamism and fragmentation, the two tendencies exemplified by the jukebox, dominated the imagery of the Populuxe era. Cities exploded outward from their centers and filled great swatches of landscape. Inside houses, walls disappeared and what had been rooms became ill-defined "dining areas," "living areas," separated by barriers that were meant to be insubstantial. In graphic art, the very thin "sensitive line," derived from the work of Paul Klee, was used to define forms that appeared to be essentially weightless, and in the home, imitation wrought iron and brass-colored wire made thin drawings in the air that turned out to be tables or salt and pepper shakers. Sometimes very flimsy-looking bases were used to hold up very heavy objects, making an apparent mockery of gravity.

The entire environment had an image of open-endedness, in which things were without close connection with one another. One paradigm of this world view might be a Saul Steinberg drawing, with a distant horizon, wispy figures here and there and objects placed arbitrarily and drawn out of scale, with a lot of identical images put in with a rubber stamp. Another paradigm might be the three-dimensional movies of the early 1950s, in which objects float before

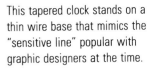

This tapered clock stands on a thin wire base that mimics the "sensitive line" popular with graphic designers at the time.

the viewers' eyes and always threaten to fall out of the screen. Although 3-D was a short-lived fad because the movies tended to be dull and cause headaches, the aural version of it, stereophonic sound, came along in 1956, and stayed. In the early days of stereo, enthusiasts turned their living rooms into drag strips, parade grounds, railroad crossings, and imagined that all sorts of noisy and unpleasant objects were making their way from speaker to speaker. The phonograph moved quickly from being something that produced tinny, unrealistic sounds to a machine producing sounds more vivid than reality itself. Stereo permitted a new dimension of vicarious experience. You could watch a cattle stampede on television, but in stereo you could feel it in the pit of your stomach. Even musical recordings engaged in sound effects, as instruments moved back and forth across the room or engaged in percussive dialogues. It is understandable that this should have happened, because stereo changed the way recordings sounded, and it did so in a way that was entirely in keeping with the expansive sense of space that was so evident in the visual realm.

This sense of airiness and freedom was most positively and successfully expressed by Alexander Calder's mobiles—probably the most popular phenomenon of fine art of the Populuxe period. Calder did his first mobiles during the 1930s, but it was in the 1950s that they were widely understood and embraced. Calder was a third-generation public sculptor. His grandfather and father did great civic works that through either representation or allegory sought to dramatize the importance and permanence of the city. With the mobile, the third Calder managed, paradoxically, to monumentalize the scatteredness of the society and the mutability of its arrangements. Most of Calder's mobiles were executed in bright primary colors, and though the tones and combinations lacked the luridness and artificiality of Populuxe combinations, their color made them very engaging. Likewise, the shapes of which they were made were abstract, but it was not a threatening or difficult kind of abstraction. For most viewers, the actual shapes themselves were not as important as their balance and movement. Besides, the same kind of abstraction was well established as part of the visual vocabulary of advertising, magazines and books of the period.

Calder's mobiles fit into another trend of the time; they were so ingratiating that people wanted to make them themselves. Indeed a lot of people probably made mobiles who had never even heard of Calder. With some coat hangers and colored paper and cardboard, the art teacher or camp counselor was able to come up with an activity that captured the imagination. It is very difficult to do a good mobile, but someone who has little artistic talent can have a good time making one. The results can often be surprising, which is fun, and movement and energy, which are difficult for an amateur to capture in most artistic endeavors, are built into the form. It was a perfect artistic expression for its time, a composition of small, visually light, separate parts connected with almost invisible materials, hanging, not standing, in precarious balance. And most important of all, the composition appears to be always changing.

Alexander Calder was the most accessible of artists. This two-year-old visitor to the Guggenheim Museum's Calder retrospective plays with his "Spider" as she might well have played with the kind of mobile that was sold for babies' cribs.

It may be that a kind of mobile was the first thing that millions of Americans ever saw. Brightly colored, plastic-covered mobiles were manufactured in the shapes of birds, butterflies and such, and they were hung over cribs. Breezes or grandparents would shake them around, engaging the babies' interest and presumably diverting their attention from their desire to be picked up. This was believed to be educational. It probably was.

Thus did the mobile enter the consciousness from the cradle and extend to the lobbies of corporate buildings and the temples of high culture. Mobility was a national obsession, and the most unlikely products took their imagery from aviation and automobiles. Exner's forward-leaning look was adopted by Eberhard Faber for its line of pencil and typewriter erasers. They went from a rectangular cross section to one that was a parallelogram, which gave them the look of always being ready to put things right. Arrow Wax was said to be more effective on the kitchen floor because it contained "jet age plastic." Radios became plastic and became two-toned. Soon they were advertised as having "sports car styling." The fellow in the ad was wearing a two-toned shirt that matched the radio. Harley Earl had spun off his own consulting firm, and his clients were able to use his association with dream cars to lend some glamour to their more stationary products. His forward-leaning design for a microfilm reader won praise in a 1959 poll of industrial designers, which had not included any of Earl's automobile designs among its most admired objects. People were aware that they were living in the jet age that was rapidly becoming the space age. Nothing was standing still. It was an age of speed, power and the excitement these engendered.

Moreover, the jet plane quickly evolved into a symbol not just of physical speed but also of social change that was believed to be happening faster than ever before. The very short time that had elapsed between Kitty Hawk and the step into space was a journalistic refrain, and some of the difficulties people have in dealing with such rapid change were suggested by Tex Avery's 1953 M-G-M animated cartoon *Little Johnny Jet*. This film, an Oscar nominee, which tells the tale of a family of airplanes, combines the sonic boom with the baby boom and dramatizes the often disconcerting combination of wonder, envy, fear and resentment that parents might have felt when confronted with their confident, fortunate children. The airplane father, a straight-winged, streamlined, propeller craft, is sitting around the hangar, reminiscing about World War II, when he notes that his wife is knitting little things. Yes, she is expecting, and after several months, when the offspring arrives it is, contrary to every genetic expectation, a jet. Johnny, as he is called, is all sharp lines and delta wings, with a cute little needle nose. Father, who has been feeling insecure about these speed-demon whippersnappers, is distraught and despondent. Then the plot takes a sort of all-mechanical John Henry turn when Dad rashly enters an around-the-world speed competition against much faster planes. Johnny comes to the rescue by towing his father to the finish line ahead of the pack. The result is that Johnny's parents win a government contract to produce many more planes just like Johnny. Mother resumes her knit-

ting. The children might be upsetting, but the hope was that they would come through for their parents and be all right after all. (The same director also made a similar cartoon, *One Cab's Family*, which was about a young hot rod who didn't want to grow up to be a taxicab like his father.)

All forms of transportation had jet age transformations, including the least likely one of all, the shoe. Aerodynamics have little to do with the efficiency of a shoe, whose form has traditionally been determined by that pre-jet age phenomenon, the foot. Shoes were also associated with a rather antique activity— walking. There was little glamour in walking during this period, and with the nearly universal use of the automobile, the average American did not have to do very much of it, but there was still a need for shoes. Advertising for men's shoes merely made the association with advanced forms of travel. A jet plane stood in the background, with a man's shoe in the foreground, just as if it were a Chevrolet. The shoes were not especially jetlike. The goal was simply to make the association between shoes and mobility as it was then understood.

It was different with women's shoes. During the mid-1950s, these went through the same transformation as the jukebox and the Plymouth. In 1954, they were rounded and compact in their appearance. In 1956, a shoe of the same size was noticeably longer. The toes were pointed, and in profile the foot rose upward in a more or less continuous line, just like a car with tailfins. The

Color, portability, and dynamic styling went hand-in-hand at the beginning of the space age. Asymmetry and two-toning made portable televisions, phonographs, and radios look lively and new, just as Little Johnny Jet's sharp shape made his rounded, propeller-driven parents feel like antiques.

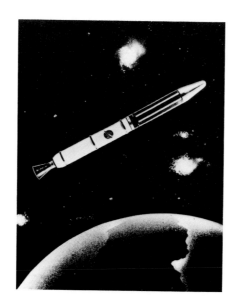

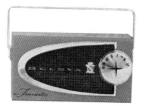

tips of the toes were empty, of course, because human feet do not come to so small a point. So was most of the extra length of automobiles. In both cases, practicality was subordinated to the need for a sharp, wedgelike profile. One difference between cars and shoes was that although both sought to look longer, lower was not a goal for shoes. Instead, their lightness was dramatized by making the heel ever narrower and more spikelike. Lightness of structure was an important visual motif of the period, and it was certainly apparent in women's shoes. The very precariousness and impracticality of the style was also an important part of its appeal. It reinforced the image of women as glamour girls who were freed from drudgery by their push-button kitchens. A woman was an adornment to her husband. She was not likely to strike out on her own in those shoes.

The fashion for pointed toes and spike heels did not originate in this country, but in Milan and Paris. Italy was the ultimate source of several characteristically Populuxe shapes and images. And the shoes were conceived as part of ensembles which used the same angular dynamic motifs one could find on automobiles and other design objects. But for the most part, gowns with jet-image capes, asymmetrical outlines and bold, free-form patterns remained in the world of haute couture. The fashion ideas that were taken up by the masses stressed informality most of the time, and elegant simplicity for occasions which were clearly formal. Bridesmaids' dresses adopted the Populuxe color palette, but rarely the dynamic lines associated with many other design objects. Nevertheless, the pointed-toe jet age shoes became nearly universal for dressy occasions, and they had an amazingly long run in this country. They came in shortly after the tailfin really took off and stayed in style until about the time the fin receded into the back of the car.

It is unlikely that any woman putting on her spike-heeled shoes was consciously thinking about their affinity to jet fighter planes. But she did have an overall sense that they were not merely what someone had said was in fashion that year, but that they really did look modern. They were in tune with the shapes and the aspirations of the times.

Another look that was closely associated with women's fashions was the sheath shape, a long cylindrical profile strongly tapered in the middle. The sheath dress was a fashion standard for several years. The shape went beyond women's fashion, however, and even appeared as the silhouette of the door handle of the Frigidaire. It served as an evocation of what was called modern elegance. It is a shape one finds in the legs of some Danish furniture, the outlines of newel posts in stairways of modern buildings, giving both a vaguely anthropomorphic suggestion while avoiding ornament. One finds the shape in tall salt and pepper shakers, and, with a somewhat larger, more matronly upper portion, in bottles of liquid cleansers and dishwasher detergent. If recollections of Marilyn Monroe, Jayne Mansfield and Dagmar were parked out front in the driveway, hints of Audrey Hepburn and the model Suzy Parker were standing on the stairway, at the refrigerator, on the dining table, under the sink.

The single shape that is unquestionably the most characteristic of the pe-

Women's shoes took on longer, sharper lines. The pointed toes were as hollow as tailfins, and they stayed in style for about the same amount of time.

riod is the pointed boomerang, a form that could be found on fabric patterns, floor lamps, coffee tables and corporate logos. Formica used the shape in many of its patterns. Handles of cabinets and pulls of drawers, which had typically followed a simple curved form in 1952, developed a bend by 1958. Advertisements would show jet planes leaving vapor trails in a succession of boomerang shapes. On roadside signs and in graphics, the form would often turn into a very wide, very shallow shaftless arrowhead, pointing the way to the milk shakes or the bowling alley.

The sheath shape was a continuing theme in women's fashion, but it could also be found in such consumer products as this Revlon "Futurama" lipstick. Sheath-shaped women were used in 1957 to sell the new square-cornered "sheer look" appliances.

Perhaps its definitive expression was the Chrysler Corporation logo. It was adopted for the 1955 model year to symbolize the "Forward Look," and it consisted of two boomerang shapes, one an acute angle, the other an obtuse angle superimposed. At first they were pointing directly to the right, but for the 1959 models, the logo marked the high point of the tailfin and recognized the advent of the space age by taking an upward turn. It is interesting that while the 1955 Chrysler Corporation cars were written about in many different magazines from many different angles, even advertising publications passed over the new logo and didn't feel obliged to explain what it meant. It was an instantly recognizable symbol of dynamism and of flight. Vestiges of that shape are still with us. The boomerang shape appears on Speedo bathing suits, where it promises fast movement, even on the larger sizes. It has survived in the logo for Delta Air Lines, where it is clearly related to the symbolism of the delta-wing jet aircraft.

The boomerang shape has numerous sources, but most of them lead back to aviation and mobility. The Chrysler logo, for example, can be read as a stylization of the geometry of the two competing wing configurations for fighter planes during the mid-1950s—the swept wing and the delta wing. Each had its advantages and drawbacks, and exemplars of each kept trading the world speed record. The boomerang shape was visible even more literally in the flying wing, a proposal to design an entire large transport or passenger craft as a single wing, without any fuselage. This design was seriously studied, and for

The Chrysler Corporation symbolized speed with superimposed boomerangs. The butterfly chair was like a drawing of a series of boomerangs.

Jet efficiency rubbed off on telephone address finders, and rocket power helped speed up automobiles.

a time in the early 1950s it seemed likely to be the shape of the future. These boomerang-shaped airplanes never went into production, but sketches were widely published and praised as a design innovation, which was as good as the same thing. The Douglas Skyray was actually produced, but very few people ever saw one up close. Like Harley Earl, they saw its picture in the paper. They also saw the flying wing.

But the parabolic curve, which clearly underlies the form of the more pointed variety of boomerang, has a design history of its own. It is a curve that expresses fundamental relationships in mathematics and physics, and it can be seen in the path of a projectile and other commonplace manifestations of gravitation. The great Catalan architect Antonio Gaudí used parabolic arches in place of pointed Gothic ones in several of his buildings in Barcelona, including the Sagrada Familia church. The parabolic arch came closer to the mainstream when it appeared in Bauhaus and other modernist European graphics during the 1920s and 1930s. In 1931, Le Corbusier's design for the Palace of the Soviets in Moscow had as its most memorable element a huge parabolic arch. If that design had been built, the 1950s and 1960s in America might well have looked somewhat different. Parabolic arches were used in aircraft hangars and other industrial buildings during World War II, both in Europe and in America. One such building, a municipal asphalt plant, was built on the East Side of Manhattan where a lot of people involved in advertising and communications were likely to see it. Many pieces of postwar modern furniture stood on metal parabolic arches, some pointing up, others down. Isamu Noguchi did a table with a somewhat pointed boomerang shape many years before it became widespread. Herman Miller, one of the leading manufacturers of American modern furniture, even had a parabola in its trademark.

The single most widespread and influential object incorporating a parabolic line was the Hardoy, or butterfly, chair, which is essentially four large wire hairpins supporting a sling which formed the seat and back. This was one of the first designs manufactured by Knoll, the other leading manufacturer of modern furniture, but it was eventually manufactured by countless others—including hordes of do-it-yourselfers in their basements. Knoll, which paid royalties to its designers, lost a celebrated copyright suit over the chair and stopped making it. But as many as five million of them were made, the overwhelming majority of them knockoffs. Unlike other pieces of classic furniture that have been copied, however, the butterfly chair was made of humble and commonplace materials, and a knockoff could be just as good as the original. Even though the chair is hard to get in and out of gracefully, it was, in a sense, the fulfillment of the modernist dream to use industrial materials simply to provide good, inexpensive furniture for the masses. During the mid-1950s, the decorating magazines were filled with competing ads for this product. One, in 1953, offered the deluxe model for $7.45 and the authentic model for $14.95, along with a high-backed variation, "The Swami Chair," also $14.95. Even by 1953 standards, this was a cheap way to furnish a room. Moreover, the slings were available in a variety of bright fashionable colors, and the form of the chairs themselves embodied lightness and informality. Owning one was an expression not of conspicuous consumption but of modern living.

The dynamic parabola could be found in a speedy-looking tomb-stone, a monumental charcoal grill, a 1958 advertising graphic, and the science pavilion at Seattle's 1962 World's Fair.

On a larger scale, a series of towers built with parabolic arches were the symbol of the United States Pavilion at the 1962 Seattle Century 21 Exposi-tion. The culmination of the parabolic arch motif, however, was Eero Saari-nen's competition-winning design for a monument in St. Louis to celebrate the westward expansion of the United States. It was not completed until 1966, after the architect's death, but it was designed in 1948 and construction began during the Populuxe period. The influential design very economically fused the period's fascination with motion and dynamism with its preoccupation with the settlement of the frontier. It was erected to symbolize the beginning of the American frontier, but it was exciting because, like John F. Kennedy, it prom-ised a new frontier. It unified all the different kinds of mobility—supersonic aircraft, spaceships, wagon trains and cross-country moving vans—that pro-vided the central motifs of American life during the Populuxe period. And even before the arch had been completed, its parabola had been repeated on a small scale in fast-food restaurants, gasoline stations, motels and other buildings that served the denizens of roadside America.

There are still other possibilities for the origin of the boomerang. Perhaps it came from a blob, though not exactly the kind that fell from outer space and terrorized Steve McQueen and his friends in the 1958 horror movie *The Blob*. Rather, it was the amoeboid form that started appearing in Alvar Aalto vases, coffee-table tops, Arp constructions, Matisse cutouts and advertising graphics during the period after the war. The British design historian Bevis Hillier has traced this shape to World War II camouflage patterns, used in air defense. In Britain, a lot of conscripted artists were put to work on camouflage, he says, and it had an impact. His argument is somewhat weakened by the fact that the Aalto vase and other prototypes of this form predated World War II, al-though much of the postwar design did have more in common with the cam-ouflage than with Aalto.

The graphic blob only came into its own, however, when it was allowed to float free against a white background. It seemed to be almost everywhere dur-ing the decade after World War II, almost always associated with products that were trying to identify themselves with modern ideas and sophisticated taste.

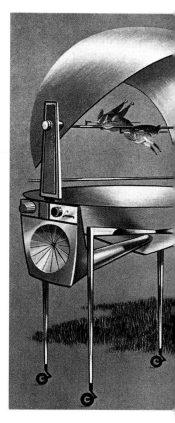

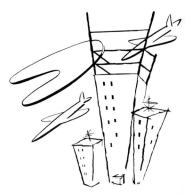

It fit in well with the widespread popularization of the visual style of Paul Klee, exploiting his thin black line, obliquely connecting bold patches of color. Blobs, and even a few near-boomerangs, were what Calder's mobiles were made of. Commercial artists were not just copying fine artists, they were sometimes hiring them. Miró, for example, did an ad for Westvāco, a container manufacturer. Some artists spanned both worlds. Ben Shahn did a lot of magazine graphics, and Saul Steinberg branched out from his work for *The New Yorker* by doing a highly acclaimed animated television commercial for Jell-O Instant Pudding. Madison Avenue did not find much it could use in the very different but significant blobs that were being made by the New York school only about forty blocks south, but they did digest and disseminate the ideas of European modernism, all in the service of selling, say, a cigar.

An important species of blob that was popular on both sides of the Atlantic was the artist's palette, often accented with dabs of color. Not only was this widespread in advertising, but it also showed up in serving dishes, tables, fabrics, and is probably also the source of the kidney-shaped swimming pool which was such a high status item at the time. The palette seems a likely progenitor of the boomerang look. A boomerang is nothing more than a palette that has been stretched and sharpened, possibly after somebody got a look at a Douglas Skyray. The boomerang could have evolved from the palette in the same way that the rounded, comfortable P-38-inspired Cadillac fins turned into the lethally sharp creations of 1959.

Another, somewhat remote source of the boomerang shape was the boomerang itself. The South Pacific was a major source of imagery during the postwar years, and this weapon of the Australian aborigines which conveniently returns to the person who throws it did gain a rather magical reputation during those times, at least among children. In 1954, there was such a demand for boomerangs, the New York *Times* reported, that aborigines had adopted assembly-line tactics in order to fight off English competition. The mystique of the boomerang was probably destroyed for good after a cereal manufacturer packed plastic boomerangs inside the box as a premium. You could throw them into the air, but they would never come back. Actually, the fact that the boomerang was supposed to come back is what most disqualifies it as the source of the boomerang shape. The form had the aura of infinite forward movement. The idea of going back where you came from never entered into it.

It is probably impossible to trace the boomerang back to just one source. It was an idea that was in the air, the result of a confluence of images that came together and were transformed by the development of jet aircraft, with its distinctive geometry of sharp angles, gentle curves and parabolic profiles. As the Populuxe period unfolded, jets gave way to spacecraft, which had an even more dartlike appearance. Products sometimes appropriated the magic of rockets simply by picturing them, as such cars as the Oldsmobile and the Chevrolet did. But some products used the form more literally. There were whiskey decanters in the shape of rockets, and pencil boxes and amusement park rides.

The rocket was the way we were going to get to the moon and other planets. The way people from other planets were getting to us was the flying saucer. The flying saucer was an ambiguous image during the period, because nobody knew whether the visitors from outer space were friendly, and people were troubled by what were widely believed to be efforts by the U.S. Air Force to cover up the interplanetary visitations and discredit those who had witnessed them. Moreover, the form of the flying saucer, which was neither streamlined in the old sense nor reflective of the new shape of motion, mocked the effort to symbolize speed. They were assumed to move in ways we did not understand, and while they were unquestionably futuristic in their connotation, they denied the technological positivism that was most characteristic of the era. Still, you can see flying saucer imagery in some mid-1950s hanging lamps and other household objects. On a larger scale, the flying saucer appeared in some roadside architecture and as a prefabricated building unit that could be used as a temporary sales office at a housing development or a booth at a parking lot. On a somewhat grander level, Philadelphia built a flying saucer visitor center in the heart of downtown, and the revolving restaurant on top of the Space Needle that served as the unofficial symbol of the 1962 Seattle World's Fair was conceived as a flying saucer from the very beginning.

Another important space age image was the starburst. It most often took

Seattle's 1962 Space Needle was an impaled flying saucer surrounded by chemical-model totems.

This freeform coffee table, a simplified blob, has an understated dynamism in its form. The center watch is also a blob, here sharpened and aggressive.

the shape of an eight-pointed star in which the vertical and horizontal points are longer than the diagonal ones. It is, in fact, the traditional compass rose, and was occasionally used with that meaning. But usually it was torn off the map and thrown into space, where it would float on products that were looking for a little class. Ford Motor Company pressed it into service as the new symbol for its top-of-the-line Lincoln. *Playhouse 90,* an ambitious series of original plays that was probably television's most self-consciously prestigious program, used a rotating three-dimensional version as its symbol. First National City Bank of New York adopted it, and Citibank still uses it. Indeed, it is embossed on some of its buildings. Metal-curtain wall panels into which the star motif was impressed were manufactured and used, for example, on the first new building ever constructed by the Sheraton hotel chain, in Philadelphia in 1957. (These were recently painted over in an effort to modernize.) And the star image is, in turn, related to, though distinct from, the asterisk look, which appeared in a lot of advertising and magazine graphics. Its ultimate realization was probably George Nelson's ball clock, which was, in effect, a giant twelve-armed asterisk hanging on the wall.

It may be, however, that the single most important and most characteristic element of Populuxe design is not any particular decorative motif but rather

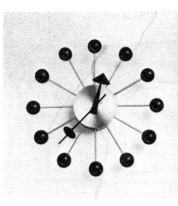

George Nelson's ball clock combined star imagery with that of the atom.

This sculptural amoeboid sofa, which pivoted on its own uphol-stered table, was described as "sinfully luxurious."

something that appears to be functional—the handle. A handle made something portable, by definition, whether or not it was possible to pick it up. The attachment of a handle to almost anything made it more informal, and more suited to the pace of contemporary life.

Furniture had become visually lighter, and rooms were more open than they had been in the past. These changes were taken to be emblematic of a society whose citizens would be open to spontaneity and change in every aspect of their lives. A visit from unexpected guests, a corporate transfer to North Carolina, all could be taken in stride by this modern flexible personality. Probably not many people actually had that personality, but they were certainly made to feel that they should. Besides, it was good for business. Women's magazine readers, especially, were subject to hortatory prose that told them about the way "we" feel nowadays. Why, they were asked, should you get bogged down with an enormous record player in one room when you might want to play a record somewhere else? Television was wonderful. You wanted to be able to take it almost anywhere. "What you've been waiting for," promised a 1957 advertisement, "Big Screen Mobility." It is unlikely that people moved their televisions and record players around very often.

And in this pre-transistor age, movement could prove to be very awkward. Televisions, which were the focus of the portability mania, were particularly

Wheeled carts and handles turned the television set into a more informal kind of product. Never mind that you couldn't pick up one of these vacuum-tube-packed portables—big-screen mobility carried the day.

heavy and ungainly objects. Their picture tubes had to be quite long, which made them bulky. Even a modest-screened television, with all its tubes, was a very difficult thing to carry around. Yet in much of the advertising for portable televisions, an elegantly dressed woman wearing white gloves is shown carrying the television, as if it were a handkerchief, with her arm completely extended. Her muscles were clearly not up to the task, and even if they were, she still wouldn't be able to do it and smile so sweetly. The television had to be nothing more than an empty box. Occasionally, there would be a drawing of a child holding, and not being crushed by, a portable television set. Children running away from home with portable television sets proved to be a durable theme for cartoonists. But real people purchasing a real television set would probably grunt and strain with it, until they got it home, hooked it up to the antenna and left it in the same place forever after.

Portability was the television industry's version of the tailfin. As with the car market, the market for television sets leveled off sharply in the mid-1950s, after a period of explosive growth. Everyone who was going to have a television set in the living room already had one. The next big boom in television sets would be brought about by color broadcasting, which was already underway. But most people were content to watch the NBC peacock in black and white until color sets became cheaper, the color became better and the other networks went to color in a big way. Meanwhile, they didn't consider their sets to be obsolete. The addition of a handle, however, turned the television into a new product, a portable television. It could be sold as a second set, for the kitchen or the bedroom. Its supposed portability made it feel less self-indulgent to have

a second set, and it also made it possible to avoid admitting who would look at it.

The handle transformed the set in another way as well. If the set was portable, it was all right for it to be in a metal or plastic case without looking cheap, because this was assumed to enhance its portability. If the television set was being bought to stand in the living room, it would have to be in a large, wooden cabinet. But a portable, however long it might stay where you put it, was just a temporary phenomenon, ready to be moved at any time, which was very reassuring.

The ideal was informality and flexibility, and new products were said to be breaking down the old patterns of living. It had already been established that people liked to eat in front of the television set. This created several options. You could buy a portable television for the kitchen. Or you might buy a two-tier end table for the living room, with a built-in snack table that slid out easily. There were chairs with built-in trays in place of one of the arms, a variation on the school desk. A proliferation of new appliances made it possible to brew the morning coffee in the bedroom or do just about anything just about anywhere.

The decorating and women's magazines delighted in taking this idea, and many others, to extremes. In 1959, *McCall's* told its readers about a family that had used small portable appliances to change their whole way of life. They had freed themselves from where things normally belong. A portable television was in the kitchen, and an electric skillet, "perfect for unscheduled parties," could be used in the family room so the hostess could cook as she entertained. There was also an electric drink mixer near Dad's chair, and over at the bar was a rather fearsome device that the magazine said would delight visitors. It was an electric hot-dog cooker. "Attach either end of the wiener to an electrode in the bottom half of the cooker. With the lid closed, current shoots through to cook the franks crisp yet juicy." They should have called it Frankenstein.

At around the same time, *Better Homes and Gardens* predicted that many homes would soon have two dishwashers, one built-in and the other portable, so it could be loaded from the dining-room table. The magazine also praised an air conditioner mounted on a cart that could be wheeled wherever in the house it was needed. It would seem to make more sense to stay with one dishwasher and use the money you save to buy another air conditioner, but that is too sensible. It was movement that mattered. And selling the product too, of course.

Just push a butto

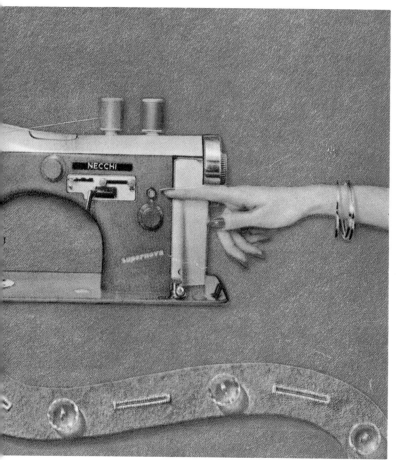

Just Push the Button

"With ordinary automatics," proclaimed a 1957 sewing machine advertisement, "you have to flip levers, twist dials, practically be a mechanic. With a Necchi, you just push a button . . ."

Clearly, by the late 1950s, America had progressed beyond the age of the "ordinary automatic." Merely saving labor was no longer a very remarkable thing. Products began to offer something more, something magical, something that could only be achieved at the press of a button. Indeed, of the terms used by people in the Populuxe era to describe their remarkable time—"the jet age," "the space age," "the atomic age"—"the push-button age" seems the most comprehensive and evocative, the one that embraces the miracles and the menace of the time.

There was a tremendous proliferation of push buttons on products during the late 1950s and well into the 1960s. Electric stoves turned into keyboard ranges, with push buttons for each gradation of temperature. Washing machines sprouted buttons that specified particular types of wash. In some automobile models, the automatic transmission selector ceased to mimic an old gearshift lever and was replaced by a series of push buttons. In the Edsel, these push buttons were in the center of the steering wheel, where the horn

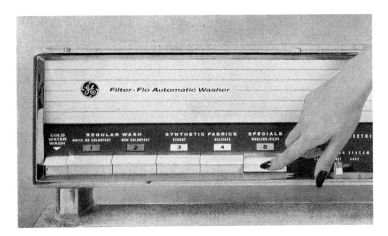

The convenient push buttons found on cars and appliances were sold as the harbingers of a glittering, effortless future.

used to be. And by the mid-1960s, electric blenders had sprouted so many buttons, each of which had a name, that it was impossible to figure out what each one did. Which beats harder, one had to ask, "liquefy" or "puree"?

In each of these instances, there was no real technological advance. The significance of the push button was entirely symbolic. It had merely replaced another kind of control device that had been doing the job satisfactorily for many years. In most cases push buttons replaced rheostat dials, which were not merely as good as push buttons for most applications but quite a lot better, since they allowed even more subtle and exact adjustment than could hundreds of push buttons. In the case of the car, push buttons replaced the transmission selection lever, which in turn had been mimicking the standard gearshift. Push buttons probably had greater practical value in cars where they replaced heat controls or the radio-tuning dial, because buttons demand less of the driver's attention than dials.

But the push button had a meaning beyond practicality or convenience. It embodied a promise. It told its user that the machine in question was competent and complex, able to do its job without any human intervention. Pushing the button was a smaller, less intimate gesture than twisting a dial. In the advertisements, if not in real life, the person pushing the button often wore dressy clothes and white gloves, which dramatized the daintiness of the little push that activated the machine and the user's lack of involvement with the drudgery to be carried out by the machine. She never seemed to have to gather and sort the dirty clothes or fill up the dishwasher with plates caked with dried egg yolk. "All you do is press the button to start the washer," Hotpoint declared. "It does the rest." Sometimes the advertisement would show a cutaway of the washing machine in which the clothes swirled in a maelstrom of detergent and rinse water. The woman doing the wash would be smiling at her children or chatting on the phone, oblivious to the turmoil she had begun with her little push.

And push buttons carried a further promise—that one day all drudgery would disappear and that almost every task that was dirty or dangerous could be carried out by unseen machinery, activated by the tiniest flick of a finger. Indeed, the adoption of push buttons for such mundane activities as adjusting the burners on the range probably grew out of the far more remarkable feats that magazines and consumer products companies promised for the future. In these technological fantasias, always backed by the authority of a research scientist or director of product development, the push of a button replaced the wave of a magic wand in fairy tales as a tool to accomplish the unlikely. Countless magazine articles and advertisements told of how you would get in your car, push a few buttons, and the car would plan its route along electronically guided, accident-free highways and get you to your destination without a bit of effort. And you would be able to use the time you save to have fun with your family. In the kitchen, the press of a button would pull a special precooked and frozen meal for each member of the family out of the freezer, send it, unseen, down a conveyor belt and into a microwave oven, which would read the code on it to know how long to heat it, and the food would finally be seen when the oven opened automatically and a steaming-hot meal would pop out.

A classic article of this genre, entitled "Push-Button Future," appeared in *Cosmopolitan* in 1958. It looked forward to 1982, and to the "gadgets that will relieve the women of tomorrow of virtually every household chore except the diaper switch." Among the inventions predicted were the ultrasonic closet, in which vibrations would rid fabrics of every particle of dirt, and the electronic vacuum cleaner, which would emerge from its own little hole in the wall at the push of a button, guide itself around the floor and go back in its hole when finished. The article noted that this machine could be used during the height of a cocktail party, because it would be programmed not to run into anything, although it does seem as if it would be somewhat unsociable to have this robotlike machine cleaning up while the guests were still there. Another vaguely unfriendly predicted household feature would be an ultraviolet ray that would be directed at visitors as they stood on the doorstep, so that they would enter the house germ-free. Dishwashers, even those with push-button controls, would be obsolete, because there would be a machine which, at the push of a button, would fabricate disposable dishes for each meal. It would be possible to alter the color scheme of your house on a whim, because the walls would be electroluminescent, charged with electricity and glowing with any color you liked. (This would be achieved with the twist of a dial, which seems a bit backward.) Your husband, an old-fashioned type, would prefer to mix his cocktails by hand, rather than electronically, and it would take him about three minutes, just about the same as it would take you to cook the turkey dinner. Before joining him for a drink, you would program the house to emit turkey-cooking aromas. "Smells wonderful," he would say, fondly.

For each of these forthcoming inventions, the author of the article quoted assurances from experts at either Westinghouse or General Electric that the scientific principle behind the product had already been established and tested. In each case, it was assumed that anything that might be technologically feasible would arrive in the American home before long. Some of the

This is your future

3D Color TV Wall Panel   Slide-back Roof   Personal Helicopter and Roof Landing Area   Moving Stairway   House-control Panel

Glass Walls   Dust-free Floors   Menu Selector and Microwave Stove   Giant-size Fruit   Ultrasonic Laundry   Electrical Heat Unit   Phono-vision Receiver

things mentioned in the *Cosmopolitan* article, such as the microwave oven and the video recorder, have done so, though television is not yet three-dimensional. But it has been some time since we have been so sanguine about the directions in which technology will drive society or about the ability of large corporations to shape the future.

One of the most striking things about that article today is what the woman, "you" in the story, would do with all the time she saved by not laboring. She would not become one of the scientists making a better life, which the article specifically said was a man's job. She would not even sell real estate. Instead, on the day described in the article, she would catch a supersonic transport that would whisk her from her home in the Chicago suburbs to Florida, to have tea with her mother. It would also get her back home in time for cocktails with her husband. The next day, she would spend the afternoon with some women friends watching a new Broadway play on the 3-D TV. All this new freedom that would come at the press of a button was really without content, and indeed, the woman would not have to be competent at anything but pushing buttons. At the end of the article, Hyman Goldberg, the author, asked an anonymous psychiatrist for his reaction. "If all or most of these things come to pass," he replied, "what I see in store for the woman of 1982 is oodles and oodles of time to lie on a psychiatrist's couch, which will tend to make her even more flabby. That'll mean she'll have to spend a couple of hours a day in a gymnasium in order to keep her figure. But of course she'll have plenty of time for that." He was right about the exercise, at least, but he seems to have stumbled upon it for all the wrong reasons.

The women who read this and other, similar excursions into the future

"Your home will be a push-button miracle ... electronic 'maids' will cook and clean by magic." So said a 1956 newspaper supplement, referring to "a time not very far away."

could, of course, compare them with their own experience. They knew that new labor-saving devices had a way of creating new labor, either by raising the standards of cleanliness women expected of themselves or by simply creating new tasks, such as preparing food for the freezer. They might have liked to fantasize about new machines that even get themselves ready and put themselves away, but they felt ambivalent about the push-button future. Housewives persistently told market researchers that although they were tired of housework, they would rather do it themselves than depend on automatic machinery. They specifically rejected the hypothetical idea of a single button they could push and accomplish all their housecleaning chores. The most likely reason for this apparent contradiction, as Betty Friedan noted in *The Feminine Mystique,* was that women feared that if they did not have housework to do, they would be left with nothing at all. They couldn't fly down to see Mother every afternoon. If their only role was as a homemaker, they wanted something to make. They told the researchers that although they did not like to scrub, they at least wanted something they could point at the dirt, obliterate it with and give them a feeling of accomplishment. Their doubts about whether they were good homemakers or merely lazy and not doing enough around the house made them purchase more and more different kinds of specialized cleansers and equipment and other housekeeping items. The push button was both a promise and a goad. It offered the hope of less drudgery and more time, but it also had the effect of promoting insecurity, which in turn sells products.

Men, too, had a say in major appliance purchases. The image of the glamorous woman pushing the button and dispatching the menial tasks of housekeeping probably appealed to the man's protective impulses and helped assuage any guilt he might have felt about not doing much around the house.

The electrical highway with self-driving cars was a persistent dream that nobody tried to make come true. Jane Jetson, in 1963, shows that pushing a button will not always produce the intended result.

But even men probably had an ambivalent feeling about the push-button future. For many people, driving an automobile is one of the most satisfying things they do. Would even perfect safety and total efficiency compensate for the loss of the experience of driving, an activity that had for decades been sold as a path to freedom, sexual pleasure and power? From time to time it would be nice not to have to pay attention as one drove, but not usually. So despite years of predictions and promises, automated, no-accident highways have never been seriously considered, and even the push-button automatic transmission proved to be a short-lived phenomenon.

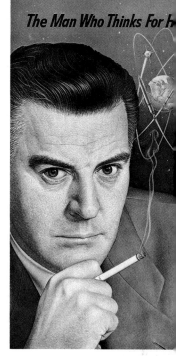

The Man Who Thinks For H

Still, throughout the Populuxe period, the term "push button" had much of the same magic that "high tech" has had more recently. It promised technological complexity, non-involvement with the technology and great convenience. But it was unnerving because it implied a certain loss of control. You pushed the button to start the process, and after that, it went its own way no matter what you did.

The imagery of the push button went far beyond the household during the Populuxe years. It was strongly tied to the military's use of computers and the replacement of manned bombers by guided missiles. Indeed, the Populuxe period linked household convenience and comfort with military strength, and the push button was the metaphor that, more than any other, forged that emotional link. Anyone leafing through a copy of *Life, U.S. News & World Report, Time* or *Newsweek* during the 1950s or early 1960s might turn from advertising for push-button washing machines and push-button transmissions to an article about how a push-button society was making America soft, and then to an account of a new computerized system for monitoring airplanes and missiles, under a headline like "Pushbutton Defense for Air War." The military was held in very high esteem during the Populuxe era. Eisenhower was a great military hero, and Kennedy won election largely on a platform of building up American military strength, which he said had been in decline. But as much as people seemed to like the military, there was little appetite for going out to fight. Americans welcomed the suggestion that national defense, too, could be put on automatic, that a few people with sophisticated machines would be able to do the entire job.

Many of the companies that were most strongly associated with consumer products—General Electric, Westinghouse, Goodyear, Chrysler—were also major defense contractors. They devoted a significant share of their advertising budgets to promotion of their military products, particularly during the late 1950s, when Eisenhower was aggressively trying to cut military expenditures and was criticizing the leaders of the armed services for their greediness. In between advertisements for Westinghouse refrigerators or light bulbs, one might find advertising for Westinghouse defense hardware. In each case, the slogan was the same: "You can be sure if it's Westinghouse."

Convenience in the household and defense of the homeland were linked. Goodyear persistently argued that greater defense spending leads to safer, more durable tires for the family car. And if the military trusted Westinghouse

to make its weapons, then it should certainly be possible to count on the company for a television set or a washing machine. And the association of household items with sophisticated military hardware made the weaponry somehow homier and more acceptable. Sometimes this identification of tools of war with life at home was taken to lengths that can only be called macabre, as when, soon after the explosion of the first hydrogen bomb in 1954, a newspaper ad proclaimed; "The Bomb's brilliant glow reminds me of the brilliant gleam Beacon Wax gives to floors. It's a science marvel."

The identification of household convenience with national strength went beyond an association of products and companies to the celebration of the entire consumer economy. Even after the terrible shock of the launch of Sputnik in 1957, there was a sense that Americans were beating the Russians through sheer buying, having and using. Americans were living so well, with such a tremendous array of conveniences, that any political system that would dare to challenge it would be foolhardy. Russians were most often depicted as poor people standing in endless lines who were unable to buy anything, and newspaper and magazine editors assumed that their readers measured their well-being by their ability to choose and purchase products.

This persistent line of American thinking reached its peak in the summer of 1959, when the United States and the Soviet Union exchanged exhibitions, in Moscow and New York, respectively. For months beforehand, newspapers and magazines anticipated the impending battle of objects and the political systems they represented. "Finally," *Newsweek* said, in summing up the confrontation, "it is a contest of two diverse ways of life—of modern capitalism with its ideology of political and economic freedom and Communism." The magazine pronounced the Soviet exhibition impressive, but rather dull, while experts it consulted called Soviet plastics good, but the plastic objects poorly designed, the steel not up to American standards, and the model kitchen efficient, but very small.

Vice President Richard M. Nixon was set to open the American exhibition, and by his account in *Six Crises,* he prepared himself carefully. He sought advice from an unidentified former ambassador to Moscow, who cautioned him: "We are idealists. They are materialists. You can no more describe Khrushchev or any other Communist as being sincere than you can describe that coffee table as being sincere." Perhaps this was so, but Nixon knew of the sincerity with which these idealistic Americans cared about coffee tables and the other objects in their lives, and much of his visit to Moscow was preoccupied with a celebration of American materialism. In his major speech there he spoke of America's 44 million families, with their 56 million cars, their 50 million televisions and 143 million radios, and noted that three-quarters of them owned their own homes. He said the United States "comes closest to the ideal of prosperity for all in a classless society."

But unquestionably, the climax of his visit was the famous "kitchen debate," which took place in a rather modest, by late-1950s standards, model suburban home that had been built by a Long Island builder in the park where

With satellites and space travel, the future had arrived. The imagery of earth orbit was new and powerful.

the exhibition was held. Nixon and Khrushchev had been walking through the exhibition, exchanging barbs, in the company of about a hundred mostly American reporters and photographers. Khrushchev repeatedly spoke of how the Soviet Union would soon catch up to the United States and leave it in its wake, while Nixon kept changing the topic to color television sets and such. Finally, when they arrived in the kitchen of the house, they began discussing washing machines, with Nixon extolling American freedom of choice while Khrushchev argued that one kind of washing machine is enough, as long as it works well. "Isn't it better to talk about the relative merits of washing machines than the relative strength of rockets?" Nixon asked. "Isn't this the kind of competition you want?" Khrushchev replied angrily that the United States was engaging in both types of competition, something that was fairly difficult to deny. Nixon and Khrushchev shook their fingers at each other photogenically as they argued.

It was an inspired piece of scene setting. Americans had been angered and shaken by Khrushchev's gruff, crude, threatening manner, and in the photographs that came back, Nixon seemed to be making a stand for American values right in the setting that was most meaningful to Americans, in the heart of the suburban house—the modern push-button kitchen. Nixon said in his book that it was all quite spontaneous, although William Safire, the New York *Times* columnist who was then in public relations, has written of the way in which he staged it. The leader of the Soviet Union was an unwitting though essential actor in this scenario staged for U.S. consumption. The images that resulted were very powerful, largely because they seemed to confirm what many Americans believed. The way they lived, with their comforts and conveniences, was shown as an essential part of the American way of life. Not only was it worth defending, but it was a defense in itself because its richness challenged every other political system, every other country, to do the same for its citizenry.

There was one curious exchange at the end of the famous debate which was discussed relatively little at the time. Khrushchev pointed to a piece of highly automatic kitchen equipment and said, "This is probably always out of order." Nixon laughed heartily and agreed in Russian: "*Da*." By this time, Nixon had had his photo opportunity, and his identification with the modern kitchen and standing up to Communism were probably secure. But this was just the sort of needling comment from Khrushchev to which he had reacted so negatively before. If Bob Hope had said it, hearty laughter might have been called for, but from the man who had threatened "We will bury you," this criticism of the reliability of American technology would seem to have been just as provocative as anything else Khrushchev said. It did speak to a real concern. During the previous two years, Americans had seen the Soviet Union launch the first satellites, land on the moon, photograph its dark side, and send far heavier payloads into space than American rockets could achieve. This had raised some doubts about the effectiveness of American technology and about the country's military preparedness. The first American attempts to match

In 1957, Americans were waiting for the Navy's Vanguard satellite to enable us to catch up with the Soviet Union's Sputnik. Here, a young space enthusiast examines the General Electric engine that promised to do the job.

"Isn't it better to talk about the relative merits of washing machines than the relative strength of rockets?" Vice President Richard M. Nixon asked during the "kitchen debate" in Moscow in 1959. Both Nixon and Khrushchev knew that Soviet rockets were more powerful, while Americans had a clear lead in automatic washers.

Sputnik were televised live, and watching American rockets rise slightly off the launching pad, then collapse in flames, threatened to become an early-morning ritual. Eventually, the tiny Explorer I was launched by the Army, and then several more, but doubts had been raised. And the year after the kitchen debate, John F. Kennedy won the presidency over Nixon after hammering away at what he termed the nation's "missile gap."

The immediate reaction to the national bout of insecurity touched off by the launching of Sputnik was overwhelming. The defeat in space was interpreted not as the consequence of a military decision not to build large, high-payload rockets but as a reflection on the American character. The United States started building bigger rockets and launching lots of satellites, of course, and by the early 1960s, these satellites began to have a direct impact on the lives of ordinary people. Science and rather militaristic technology were seen to have a payoff in the home, exactly as promised. Television programs and even telephone calls were beamed around the world almost instantaneously, and cloudy pictures taken from outer space became part of the weather forecast. The American space program was shaped as a civilian undertaking, for largely civilian aims. And the task of repenting for the failure that Sputnik represented was placed squarely on the schools. Science education was viewed as the cornerstone of American ability to keep up with the Soviets, even though it was a rather long-term investment to overcome what experts knew would probably be a short-term weakness. They did not point this out, of course, because the experts were looking for ever larger budgets and more serious commitments to space and other high technology. And there was a hunger to somehow package all pressing problems into household-size units. Making the children study their science was one satisfactory way of coping with the insecurity of life at that time, and it surely couldn't do any harm.

Even before satellites provided any services to the average American family, they had had an impact on home decoration and product design. The satellite provided a new image for the space age, one which contrasted strongly with the dynamic lines of the jet plane and the rocket. Because they move through the vacuum of outer space where they encounter no resistance, satellites do not have to be any particular shape. Compared with the rocket and the jet plane, the satellite looks non-directional and fairly ungainly. The first satellites were described and pictured as looking like a grapefruit bristling with communications antennae, and that is the image of the satellite that showed up on glasses and ashtrays, in the decor of motels and the opening titles of television newscasts.

One of the most unexpected emergences of the satellite motif was in vacuum cleaners. The last major design changes in vacuum cleaners had involved the streamlining of the Electrolux and the placement of a headlight on the Hoover upright, both of which had happened decades before. But shortly after the launch of Sputnik, Hoover came out with a spherical model, the Constellation, which was clearly inspired by satellites. Some other manufacturers followed suit, and the satellite vacuum cleaner became almost a generic type, though a rather short-lived one. (Another brand went longer and lower, with what was called "hug the floor styling." None developed tailfins.)

An idea popularized by the launching of satellites was that of earth orbit. The earliest satellites hurtled about the earth very quickly, once an hour or so, which surely set a new standard for speed in man-made objects. It was so fast that it was almost beyond representation. This gave rise to a new image of the earth, viewed as a whole, girdled by orbiting satellites moving around at impossible speeds. Such representations resulted in such products as table lamps in which the bulb emerges from an orb, around which brass hoops, defining many different planes, represent not the satellites but their various orbits. In hanging fixtures for public places, the source of light is at the center, and the orbits provide a kind of shade. The orbit was found in many advertising graphics and the full range of cheap dishes and bar ware. Some survive, mostly in family-owned coffee shops, down to the present. Although most products bearing such imagery are post-Sputnik, this vision of high-speed orbits is closely tied to another frequently depicted scientific image of the period—that of the atom with its orbiting electrons.

Satellites like *Explorer 6* had an impact on products like this Hoover Constellation vacuum cleaner.

Various forms of atomic imagery had been around ever since the atomic bomb was first used in 1945, but the use of such motifs intensified during the mid-1950s. The earliest and most pervasive was the use of thin metal rods with small colored or shiny spheres stuck at the ends, and sometimes at connections as well. In a wrought-iron bookcase, for example, the spheres could serve as feet and as decorative elements along the top. Sometimes, as in a lamp, the bulb and shade would mimic an oversized sphere at one end of a suspended or balanced rod, sometimes with a small sphere at the other end. This kind of decoration came right out of the laboratory and the chemistry class, where molecular models were built with rods and little spheres of different colors. It was seen in its most literal form in the huge atomic model that served as the centerpiece for the World's Fair in Brussels in 1958.

But the sphere-and-rod look of chemical models and drawings had a major impact on objects that had no connection with the atom. In a lattice, such a pattern could form a very transparent screen which nonetheless demarcated areas with some dignity Such screens were often used in churches and public buildings. This pattern also showed up in fabrics, on chinaware and glasses and innumerable other household objects. People in the late 1950s and early 1960s were bombarded with information about the promise of science. Atom-powered wristwatches were just around the corner, said *Science Digest*. Nuclear-powered cars that would drive themselves were not a wild dream but even now were being studied, other articles noted. Nuclear power promised to be an essential underpinning of the even better life one's children could anticipate. Nevertheless, people were acutely aware that the atomic bomb could blow everyone to smithereens or worse. During the 1950s, countless movies associated radioactivity with severe unwanted changes. In *The Incredible Shrinking Man*, the protagonist passes through an atomic cloud and soon becomes so small that his comfortable little suburban house becomes a place of menace. Atomic imagery, like the dream of the nuclear watch, was an attempt to domesticate the image of the most frightening thing around by putting it on commonplace objects.

Although atomic decorative motifs were so widespread, and often so abstract, that people did not really think about or even recognize their association, there was one common household object that was inextricably linked to the threat of nuclear annihilation—the push button. The President of the United States was widely viewed as having a push button on or in his desk that would trigger atomic war as surely and inexorably as a housewife could activate her dishwasher. And in the Kremlin there was another push button, with just about the same power. It might require a slightly more complex set of instructions to blow up the world than to turn on the dishwasher, but both were all-or-nothing gestures. "Press a button today," said *U.S. News & World Report* in an article that was clearly intended to be reassuring, "and more than 200 missiles with nuclear warheads would go speeding to specific cities in Russia. An additional 500 smaller missiles would be fired at other targets." There was no suggestion that one could push the button only partway.

The metaphorical power of the push button probably moved upward from cars and appliances to represent the plight of the President as an ultimate, if none-too-subtle, decision maker. "You don't *prepare* breakfast," an acerbic philandering husband tells his lavishly applianced housebound wife in a 1958 *Alfred Hitchcock Presents*. "You launch it like a missile." The implication was that she was both hostile and stupid, and not nearly as attractive or exciting as the women who so amused him in the city. "Do you know where I can get a warhead?" the wife replies, with just a hint of sexual provocation. Just pushing the button brings with it the implication of power, but also lack of control. Housewives said they wanted to be able at least to point their appliances toward the task, and there was a general worry about the amount of faith the country was placing in push-button warfare.

The atom was an ambiguous image. It was frightening, but it was also futuristic, and it showed up on all sorts of objects, such as this electric razor. Chemical models were the inspiration for designers worldwide. The Atomium, the centerpiece of the 1958 Brussels World's Fair, was probably the largest example ever.

"Atomburgers coming right up!" This woman is standing at a push-button range with America's first operational nuclear-power plant in the background. What she has in her skillet, so General Electric announced in 1955, are the first hamburgers ever cooked with atomic energy. People feared nuclear war, but "atoms for peace" were welcomed during the Populuxe era.

Indeed, Nixon may have been a little too quick to laugh at Khrushchev's gibe about how the appliance never works. The next year, in the election campaign against Kennedy, he had to face not only the missile gap but what seemed an almost contradictory concern: the fear of accidental nuclear war because of human or mechanical error. Kennedy argued against dependence on what he called "push-button weapons systems based on instant response." Such a concept was familiar to the public through very popular novels and movies. "The world was probably destroyed by a bunch of vacuum tubes and transistors," said Fred Astaire, playing an automobile-racing scientist waiting for the killing cloud to arrive in the 1959 film *On the Beach*. And in the 1962 novel *Fail-Safe,* made into a movie released in 1964, the President of the United States authorizes the destruction of New York City, to show the Russians that the bombing of Moscow was all an unfortunate mistake. "No human being made any mistake and there's no point in trying to place the blame on anyone," the President tells the Soviet leader, who nonetheless demands that New York be annihilated as a mark of sincerity.

In his concern about push-button warfare, Kennedy was not arguing for fewer weapons or greater peacefulness. He wanted a larger and more diverse defense establishment which would give the President a greater range of options, a choice of buttons to push, that, like a better blender, would offer the promise of carrying out its task more precisely and efficiently. Once Kennedy was elected President, however, the button, the one that would trigger nuclear war, became an ever larger preoccupation. Surely, no President ever appeared to be spending so much time hovering near it, ready to pounce. Kennedy and the button seemed a long, existentialist flirtation, one that threatened to reach its climax in the Cuban missile crisis of 1962. "If you could think only of yourself," he told William Manchester, "it would be easy to say you'd press the button, and easy to press it too." It is the nature of push buttons that they are easy to press, but the other side of that is that there is not much heroism or even dignity in doing so. The push button is a symbol of power, but it makes the person who pushes it seem a bit dumb, and even useless. Kennedy had a reaction not unlike that of the surveyed housewives—once you push the button, what then?

For a while, Kennedy actually had an answer: fallout shelters. This had the appeal of being an activist, optimistic response to a very frightening situation. It had the promise of making the all-or-nothing nature of the push button less absolute. In fact, this was a program that he took from then New York governor Nelson Rockefeller, who during 1959 and 1960 promoted a massive fallout-shelter-building program for his state. A mania for fallout shelters was in the air. The January 1960 New York Home Furnishings Show, for example, featured a bright, colorful, tastefully decorated fallout shelter that was labeled "The Family Room of Tomorrow." It had a gaily patterned sofa, a television set built into the wall and canned goods and other foods sufficient to nourish a family of five for two weeks. In October 1960, *Popular Mechanics* featured a fallout shelter in its house of the year and provided half a dozen different ways of building them. "A bomb is dropped on a key target," the article began. "But who cares, you live miles away. Fallout can't reach you. But soon, you and your family become ill, dangerously ill. Now you wish you had heeded the importance of a family fallout shelter."

And *Better Homes and Gardens*, which in 1955 had published a general's theological musings on why "God meant for us to find the atom," identified a new problem in those trying times. Canned goods left in a fallout shelter for more than a year tend to develop a metallic taste, the magazine said, and there was really nothing that could be done about that. The magazine suggested a system of rotation in which newly bought food would be put in the shelter to replace earlier purchases, which would in turn be rotated up to the kitchen for immediate consumption. Tinny-tasting tomato soup seems among the lesser risks of the nuclear age, but the magazine's concern with the topic indicates the limited extent to which it thought women would be interested in a public issue and the widespread desire to assume that the world would not be greatly changed by atomic warfare. Movies and television programs which dealt with the aftermath of nuclear war tended to promise a post-conflagration scene that was clean and pretty, though much less crowded than what went before. And just as that general told us that the atom was another divine challenge, much like the Tree of Knowledge in the Garden of Eden, popular images of a post-nuclear world seemed to revolve around a man and a woman surviving with the task of repopulating the world. In the 1959 film *The World, the Flesh, and the Devil*, the plot explores what would happen if only a woman and two men survive—and one of the men is black!

But although the notion of digging a hole from which one could emerge as the new Adam, or at least the new Noah, had been latent, July 25, 1961, marks the day on which it turned into a national mania. A few months before, an American-backed effort by Cuban exiles to invade Cuba through the Bay of Pigs had become an embarrassing debacle. The Soviet Union was putting pressure on West Berlin. And in a televised speech on the Berlin crisis, Kennedy announced a nationwide, primarily private effort to build fallout shelters. His plea did not result in the massive building of shelters, but it did generate a lot of thinking about shelters and about the fraying fabric of American society.

Perhaps the most interesting thing about the whole fallout shelter flap was the assumption behind Kennedy's program, which would have transformed civil defense from a community-based responsibility to one that was carried out by individual suburban families. Air-raid shelters were hardly a new thing, but previously they had been group facilities which mobilized the solidarity people feel when faced by common adversity. Kennedy's program, which was welcomed by the building materials and construction industries, foresaw the fallout shelter as yet another feature of the suburban home. It was something more to be added, another room to be sold, another way of convincing the buyer to spend more money on housing. And the family, not the community, became the key unit of survival. This was so clear a reflection of the way in which American society perceived itself at the time that the novelty of the approach was scarcely noticed.

Almost immediately, however, some new and disturbing social and ethical questions arose. What about those irresponsible people who failed to provide shelters for themselves and then wanted to get into your shelter, which would be equipped with only enough provisions for your own family? If you admit your improvident neighbor, you might doom your family and yourself. Maybe you should have a gun in your shelter, to make sure that your neighbors don't imperil your safety. In one very celebrated and controversial article in the Catholic magazine *America,* L. C. McHugh, a Jesuit priest and former teacher of ethics at Georgetown University, outlined "the grim guidelines of essential morality at the shelter hatchway." He argued that allowing neighbors into the shelter was morally equivalent to squandering your family's resources by giving them to a needy stranger—irresponsible charity. And if neighbors sought by force to enter one's shelter, this could be considered an unjust attack, and force could legitimately be used, provided that it is not more force than is necessary to achieve its purposes. He said the Christian act to help one's neighbor is not admitting him, threatening the lives of all, but helping him to build a shelter of his own. But he did not suggest any community-wide cooperation that could lessen the tensions among neighbors.

The response to this article and the issues it raised overflowed into many different publications and media, because the dilemma outlined truly revealed what kind of a society America had become. In John Cheever's short story "The Brigadier and the Golf Widow," Pastern, a vociferous country club cold warrior,

After President Kennedy called for the building of private fallout shelters, nearly every good Democratic politician posed for his picture in one. Here, Pennsylvania Governor David Lawrence goes a step further by adding a rocking chair, another Kennedy-inspired fad.

The well-equipped shelter had cigarettes, baked beans, parcheesi, a radio (though nobody knew who might be broadcasting)—and a shovel.

sees his life ruined by his rash decision to give the woman with whom he is having an affair the key to his fallout shelter. But she is not the only one wheedling for admittance. There is also a bishop who shows so much interest in the shelter when he comes by for a visit with Mrs. Pastern that she wonders: "Was it impious of her to suspect he was travelling around his domain picking and choosing sanctuaries? . . . The burden of modern life, even if it smelled of plastics—which it seemed to—bore down cruelly on the supports of God, the Family, and the Nation. The burden was top-heavy, and she seemed to feel the foundations give."

The debate over shelter-door morality placed the fragility of American civilization in sharp relief. Americans seemed almost eager to crawl into little holes in the ground and emerge into a simpler, less populated world. Nuclear holocaust had been redefined as a radical form of suburbanization by other means. "I really wonder if our interest is so much in survival as in the fascinating possibility we might be legitimately able to get rid of our neighbors," Frederick E. Jessett, an Episcopal clergyman from South Dakota, wrote in

Christian Century. "If we really want to be safe, we'd better start shooting our neighbors now, to be sure we get them all."

Fewer than six months after Kennedy had set off this terrifying inquiry into the values of his countrymen, he called it off. "Let us concentrate on keeping enemy bombers and missiles away from our shores and less on keeping neighbors away from our shelters," he said. The shelter program continued officially, and exploration of the concept of community shelters was added to it. But essentially, the fallout shelter craze, which had prompted far more introspection than excavation, was over. Nobody in public life would soon forget the revelation that the American public had been atomized on its way to becoming the great mass market. Traditional loyalties had been shattered. Families, now dispersed and highly mobile, were seen as being on their own, divorced from any larger community. There was no button to be pushed that could turn a country full of consumers into a cohesive body of responsible, public-minded citizens.

Lost in Space

"Less is more."

—Ludwig Mies van der Rohe, architect

"Let's just say you like ice cream. Why have one
scoop of ice cream? Have three scoops."

—Morris Lapidus, another architect

Mies van der Rohe and Morris Lapidus both reached the peaks of long careers
in architecture during the Populuxe years. Mies made ever more refined, ever
more abstract rectangular compositions of steel and glass, in his famous apartment towers and Crown Hall in Chicago and in the Seagram Building in New
York. Lapidus built great glitzy hotels in Miami Beach and elsewhere, buildings that did everything they possibly could to knock their visitors' eyes out.
They represent extreme positions in architecture. Mies the ascetic, seeking
perfection through the reduction of the elements of architecture, seems light-
years removed from Lapidus, who laid on everything he could think of in order
to please as many people as possible. Each enjoyed considerable success dur-

ing the 1950s and early 1960s. Mies and Lapidus were, respectively, the superego and the id of American architecture during a time when America's image of itself was experiencing profound change. They seemed to define the limits of the possible. But they did have some things in common. They were both working with modern technology and, more important, with a modern perception of space, place and how the entire environment should be made.

Only Lapidus could be labeled Populuxe, of course. Indeed, the Fontainebleau Hotel in Miami Beach might stand as the definitive Populuxe monument. From the moment Lapidus's client told him, "I want that nice modern French provincial," it seemed destined to be a perfect embodiment of the zeitgeist. Lapidus transformed Miami Beach, and his hotels determined the character of what became the country's most popular resort. Moreover, even though Morris Lapidus did not become a well-known name in architectural circles until the late 1960s and 1970s, his work was widely copied in the hotel industry, restaurants, retailing and commercial design in general. Suspended ceilings with free-form holes, great sweeping stairways to nowhere, curving passages to splashes of light and color, balustrades with slender sheath profiles—these were the clichés of the 1950s, and Lapidus invented most of them. He was using many of them in the design of retail stores as early as 1931. The very thin metal verticals, used as structure, separation or modulation, he referred to as bean poles. The floating ceilings with openings he called cheese holes. And the free-form, palette-into-boomerang shape he called the woggle. Bean pole, cheese hole and woggle just about summarize the popular design vocabulary of the Populuxe era, and Lapidus used them first, with a boldness and bravura that were unexcelled.

A woggle with cheese hole, suspended from bean pole.

Mies was far better known during the Populuxe period than Lapidus, and he was certainly a much more important role model to architects who considered themselves to be serious. His principal effort was to use the materials of machine age construction—the steel girder and the sheet of glass—as the elements of an architecture that would achieve for modern times an order different from, but equivalent to, that of the classical tradition in architecture. The glass box, too, became a cliché during the Populuxe era. While Lapidus's clichés covered the buildings made for fun, recreation and personal consumption, Mies's clichés were applied to the high-rise office tower, the municipal building, the subsidized housing project. Mies's impersonal architecture was used for impersonal buildings, ones which did not have to compete to please customers.

The formal experiments in which Mies was engaged may have interested other architects in the discipline and expression of the glass box, but they were not the real reason for the proliferation of such buildings around the country. The unadorned glass-and-steel structure could be built very cheaply. It was not cheap to build a Mies building, because his works were luxuriously detailed and finely crafted, but it was cheap to build a steel-framed glass box that looked vaguely Miesian. Before World War II, modernism in architecture had been a cause for relatively few. But the war had forced a number of the pioneer modernists out of Germany, and some were given powerful positions in American schools. Walter Gropius, head of the Bauhaus, which pioneered the impersonal industrial aesthetic, took over the architecture department at Harvard, and by the early 1950s the clean lines and reformist rhetoric of international modernism were architectural orthodoxy. But even many of those who were modernist apostles or propagandists would agree with the assessment of Philip Johnson, Mies's most famous advocate and sometime collaborator, that most such buildings were produced cynically, to cut down on expense.

It was important that most architecture be inexpensive, because nobody cared very much about architecture. Architecture deals best in collective expression; this was a time of private indulgence. Companies understood that image building could be accomplished far more effectively and flexibly with national advertising than by erecting a landmark building in its headquarters city. Most lavish corporate headquarters buildings of the time were, in fact, in the modernist style, because this was identified, by the upper middle class at least, with progressiveness and efficiency. The well-functioning machine was viewed as a reasonable model for corporate life. It was believed that public buildings, traditionally the most substantial and lavishly ornamented of structures, should be efficient and, therefore, modern, but they didn't have to be grand. People preferred to pay lower taxes and save the grandeur for their own living rooms. They would turn out at community meetings to keep their school boards from "building the Taj Mahal," often because higher taxes would make it harder for them to afford their own homes.

Even the works of Lapidus, which were intended as evocations of luxury and opulence—once-in-a-lifetime experiences—were built relatively cheaply, according to the businesslike standards of the time, and then embellished. Like mass-produced furniture, in which applied ornamentation is able to cover up poor joinery, Lapidus's buildings used a lot of sparkle to divert the eye from often boring and ungainly structures. In Mies's buildings, where the vocabulary was so restricted, each detail had to be exquisite, which made them much more expensive. But what makes Mies and Lapidus such an interesting contrasting and overlapping pair is not their use of the materials and the detailing of modern architecture, but the way in which they dealt with the phenomenon of modern space.

In 1929, at an international exhibition in Barcelona, Mies designed a building for Germany which was remarkable for such an enterprise because it seemed not to contain anything. All it held was something that most people had never experienced—a new way of looking at space and at the world itself. The interior was open, but interrupted by non-structural walls that modulated the way the space flowed through the building. Mies's openness was altogether different from that which had been advocated by Frank Lloyd Wright. All of Wright's houses had some form of open plan, but in these the space was typically energized by two axes, crossing at a central hearth. They were highly directional, and their form was strongly influenced by the landscape, which they generally sought to embrace rather than command. In short, they expressed something about family life, about the desire to move and the desire to be rooted. They had meaning beyond themselves. The message of the Barcelona pavilion and other Mies works was, by contrast, that there was no larger meaning.

Wright's houses built in the Chicago suburbs around the turn of the century had transformed architecture and helped trigger modernist architecture in Europe. In 1951, Mies completed a house outside Chicago that was a far less complex artistic statement than Wright's prairie houses and thus, it seemed, clearer and more up-to-date. It was the Farnsworth house, which still exists but, like the Barcelona pavilion, is primarily known through a small group of very beautiful photographs. It is a glass box that seems to float in a field, shimmering and totally abstract. Hovering above the grass and the flowing creek, the house appears to exist on a plane of pure reason. Its values are not of this world, and it is not linked to the earth. The architect merely marked out a patch of the earth with his ruler, and on that patch, he made art. As art, it is compelling, but as a house, arbitrary, a glass box that, while visually open to nature, is sealed and, therefore, functionally windowless. It actually denies the power of the natural world and the traditional responsibility of architecture to shelter its inhabitants from the elements. The owner of the house became embroiled in a legal battle with the architect, claiming that it was uninhabitable, and she wrote an article in *House Beautiful* to caution readers not to let such a thing happen to them.

Mies's pavilion at Barcelona was an essay in flowing space, sumptuously interrupted.

The Farnsworth house in Plano, Illinois, was controversial from the moment it was finished. It was beautiful, but the owner was probably right when she said it was uninhabitable. Its kitchen was hardly homelike.

Some religious buildings were monumental, such as Frank Lloyd Wright's Beth Sholom Synagogue in Elkins Park, Pennsylvania, completed in 1958, but most were inexpensive and not too different from a gasoline station or a town hall.

The article, and the magazine's editorial that went along with it, brought a tremendous response. Wright wrote a letter of praise for the magazine's condemnation of the house and the approach to architecture it represented, as did architects from many regions of the country. The letters called for an architecture based on American living patterns, on the physical qualities of the site, the climate and the local materials. From the intellectual centers of the East Coast and Chicago came denunciations that the magazine was spreading ignorance and trying to destroy the great art of the time. The debate between the American, landscape-based sense of openness versus the international, abstract sense of openness has been one of the long-running intellectual feuds of all time. Tom Wolfe's *From Bauhaus to Our House* was a late entry on the American side, while a 1985 critical work on Mies equates the criticism of the Farnsworth house with the Red scare tactics of Senator Joseph McCarthy during the same period. It is probably fair to say that most Americans were sentimentally on the side of Wright and his more sheltering kind of architecture. But although Wright argued that it was possible to build houses sensitive to the landscape on a large scale and at moderate prices, his ideas were never really tried. But because people knew his work only from photographs, some developers were able to take bits and pieces of Wright and incorporate them as "features" on mass-produced houses. The characteristic architecture of the Populuxe period, therefore, follows neither Mies's icy abstractions nor Wright's more organic approach, but rather yet another visual approach that grew out of modernism—that of collage.

The idea of modern space had been developing for at least a century, as ways in which people understood their surroundings and symbolized the world changed drastically. First, the arrival of iron-frame construction in such buildings as London's Crystal Palace of 1851 freed buildings from the discipline that masonry structure had imposed. Suddenly, the whole idea of walls and windows could be re-examined and redefined, and the heroic engineering of churches and other buildings lost its power because such effects could not be achieved routinely. Then systems of rapid movement, first the train, then automobiles and airplanes, changed the way in which people saw their surroundings. People could see more things in a shorter time, but they would certainly see less of them. Mass transportation changed cities, making them somewhat less dense residentially, more dense commercially, while allowing them to sprawl and give over ever more of their land to individual private houses.

Such changes in the structures of buildings and cities had a parallel in the breakdown at the turn of the century of the ideal of Renaissance perspective and the emergence of cubism in painting and sculpture. Cubism, which sought to represent a number of vantage points in the presentation of an object, made viewers conscious of their own freedom in space. Right over there is just as valid a place to be as here, or very far away. Paris, where cubism emerged, is about as hierarchical a city as it is possible to find, but even there, such machinery of modernism as the Métro was suggesting the possibility of other orders to the city, other points of view. In America, the abstract non-hierarchical grid had long ago set the pattern for city and countryside alike, and the centuries of limitations that had given European cities their shapes affected only a few of the older cities. A culture which throughout its history had been preoccupied with the vastness of its own empty spaces was probably predisposed to accept a new formulation of space itself.

And then came the movies, radio and television, which carried the mes-

Bruce Goff's Redeemer Lutheran Church in Bartlesville, Oklahoma, was an attempt to make the space-age suburban church something special.

Morris Lapidus's hotels were a stylistic hodgepodge, designed to make guests feel like stars. Opposite: The entrance to the Eden Roc in Miami Beach. Above: Satyrs in expressionistic niches give an Eden Roc meeting room a piquant mixture of pretense and vulgarity. Left: the Fontaine-bleau's famous stairway to nowhere.

sage that what you experienced had nothing to do with where you were. The movie down the street brought images of all over the world, all times in history, filtered through the special sensibility of Hollywood. Television made this far more dramatic by bringing into people's houses a succession of experiences that they found as intense and vivid as life itself. And you didn't have to be in New York or anywhere. Your little raised ranch on the cul-de-sac was plugged in.

The intellectual concept of modern space thus provided a very compelling analogy to the social, technological and economic changes of postwar America. Cities became identified with old-fashioned values, a hierarchical class structure, lack of space and freedom. The suburbs were new and free, there was no declaration of hierarchy, they were informal and seemed not to exclude anyone. "Our houses are all on one level, like our class structure," *House Beautiful* declared in 1953. The development of the suburbs tended to blur distinctions between one place and another, something that was quite acceptable at the time because it vastly expanded the amount of space in which one could consider oneself to have "made it." And in this environment, people tended to think of things in terms of how long it took to drive from one place to another, rather than about the connections between them. Mass communications and personal transportation had vastly expanded people's concept of space and changed their view of what was in the space.

This sense of infinite space, of the separation of people and objects in it and the tenuousness of the relationships, can be seen in all sorts of creations of the mid-twentieth century, from philosophy to advertising graphics. It is an expression of social fragmentation, perhaps, of a loss of belief, of the discoveries of science that almost everything that appears to be solid is made up almost entirely of emptiness and of tiny particles bound with immense energy in almost inconceivable motion. It is into this empty landscape that Samuel Beckett puts his tree. Existentialists stood in this nowhere with the resolution to *do something,* absurd as it might be. Beatniks hitchhiked through it; families packed up the Chevrolet and sped through it. And Morris Lapidus built resort hotels there.

"They weren't essentially cultured people," said Lapidus of the people who stayed at his Miami hotels. "Some of them may have been, but they'd forgotten their culture." In his book *The Architecture of Joy,* Lapidus, who came to the United States as a boy from Russia, recounts his ghetto upbringing and his overwhelming desire to be accepted by the society at large. In designing the Fontainebleau, he realized that the culture to which the clientele was aspiring was the only one they could know—that presented in the mass media, and especially the movies. That meant they wouldn't be schooled in how the grand buildings of the past were put together, nor would they be interested. They

The Eden Roc (1955) and the Fontainebleau (1954) are both standard modern buildings that have been dressed up. Lapidus used lots of curves, inside and out, to soften the Eden Roc's boxiness.

would have no particular expectations based on traditional proportions, historic styles or particular building materials or construction methods. Instead, they would want to see things in person that reminded them of things they had seen in films. "All through the interior is a potpourri of anything I could get my hands on," he said of the Fontainebleau. "My palette has materials and stylistic things left over from the past. I use them any way I want. They have no interrelationship." The massive clientele for Lapidus hotels was made up of a kind of person who had never before been present in such numbers—lower-class people who had recently acquired enough money to really indulge themselves. "I designed what I did for *them:* the immensity of a meaningless lobby; the overabundance of beautiful antiques; the feeling of great opulence. When they walk in they *do* feel, 'This is what we've dreamed of, this is what we saw in the movies, this is what we imagined it might be.'"

Lapidus likes to sum up his work with the aphorism "A hotel should be no place like home." His hotels very literally evoke a special kind of no place, one remembered vaguely from a whole lot of filmed fantasies. He let people walk into the glamour of the movies, let them perform and be stars for a little while. He was criticized by his fellow architects and by critics for his belief in embodying illusion, which led, it was argued, to kitsch values replacing reality and to the debasement of the entire culture. Lapidus pleaded guilty as charged to using kitsch elements, but he often pointed out that it was probably not wise to look for Miami Beach hotels to carry the flame of the future of civilization. They involved serious financing, he said, but not serious architecture. During

the Populuxe years, serious architecture was aggressively reformist, often in a rather dictatorial way. For many architects, the phenomenon of modern space provided an opportunity to erase all that had gone before and start anew. But even very good architects who tried to create whole new environments tended to produce places that were sterile and frightening. There was nothing liberating about being lost in space.

It may be that while serious architects were still digesting the changes of the nineteenth century and refining their responses, Lapidus and a lot of other commercial architects and developers were dealing in a quick, crass but sometimes inspired way with the changes of the twentieth. Which has more impact: a steel girder or an image on a television screen? There's no comparison. Even if the image on the television screen is of a steel girder, its appearance on the screen gives it greater importance than anything to be found in mere reality. And Lapidus's clients, who were smart about hotels but uneducated about architecture, forced Lapidus to think about the people who would use the buildings. At that time, most architects still thought in terms of a society with a few wealthy and powerful patrons, but the real wealth of the society was to be found in the paychecks of millions of working people—the ultimate patrons of the Fontainebleau.

Lapidus's San Souci has a canopy like a tongue, which continues far into the lobby.

Lapidus created buildings that to an educated eye, including his own, had a good deal of the ridiculous about them. Tonguelike cantilevered concrete canopies at the entrances have a way of sweeping forward a little bit too far and then going still farther. Lobbies are enormous, but the chandeliers still manage to be a little bit too large for them. The designs induce people to walk around, not so much by any sophisticated modulation of the space, as in baroque architecture, but by having statuary, fountains, lights and views appear at regular intervals along gently curving paths, rather like billboards or drive-in restaurants along the highway. His spaces are not a single experience that builds and develops. Rather, they are organized by the more familiar and accessible pattern of one thing after another.

At the Fontainebleau he designed uniforms for the staff that had a touch of Ruritania to them, and he had the room furniture made oversized to give an aura of importance and luxury to the whole experience, even though it's all pretty silly if you look at it critically. He was quite ready to point out, even as he was disclaiming seriousness, that a few of these tricks had been successfully in places like St. Peter's in Rome. He compared his frank desire to please an uncultured or culturally forgetful clientele to that of the Catholic Church, which he said had used impressive architecture as a way of inducing the masses to believe. He said that he was similarly preparing people to enjoy themselves: "You want to have fun. Don't try. You are in my hotel. You're having fun. You're having a ball; this is the greatest experience of your life. Poor fellow doesn't know if he's enjoying himself or not. But I've set it for him. He *is* enjoying it."

Lapidus went as far as an architect could go in making a place the masses could enjoy. But some others, who were not architects, went even farther. In

Miami Beach, Lapidus made spaces like the ones in the movies, but outside Los Angeles, some moviemakers made a place that was like walking into a movie. More than any architects, they understood the way in which the movies and television changed the nature of experience itself, and they created the greatest of all pieces of Populuxe architecture—Disneyland, which opened in Anaheim, California, in 1955. Disneyland was the first place ever conceived simultaneously with a television series, and the geography of Disneyland was known by millions of people all over America even before the place existed. There had been amusement parks before, of course, but there had never been anything quite like Disneyland, a whole and perfect place, a Magic Kingdom off the highway, a recognizable somewhere in the middle of nowhere in particular.

Disneyland was, of course, Walt Disney's idea, and he stayed within his close-knit organization to get the project designed and built. He gave the designers of Disneyland the title "imagineers," but for the most part, these were the same people who had given the world Mickey Mouse, *Snow White, Dumbo* and *Fantasia*. They did not think as architects; they were filmmakers. And what they designed was not a group of buildings or a park but an experience. They thought in very literally cinematic terms as they designed the place as a movie that could be walked into. As animators, they had begun with storyboards which established how the experience would unfold, and they did the same thing as "imagineers." Walking through Disneyland, one unavoidably experiences a series of long establishing shots, medium shots and close-ups. And in keeping with the Disney style, they thought about the things one feels very proud of noticing, just out of the corner of one's eye. It usually turns out, in the films as in the theme park, that everyone else has noticed them and felt proud too. But the density of the experience, the fact that it always seems as if

Walt Disney himself ushers Vice President Richard M. Nixon, his wife, Pat, and their daughters, Julie and Tricia, onto the Disneyland monorail in 1959. Disneyland's "House of the Future" opened in 1957 but was torn down a decade later.

there is almost too much to see, is perhaps the chief component of the Disney magic.

You can't believe your eyes in Disneyland, and of course you shouldn't. Everyone knows that the hippopotamus, the crocodile and the headhunters seen in the famous jungle ride are fake, but they probably don't think too much about things like stone walls. Disneyland could have afforded to use real materials, but in many cases, it has chosen not to do so. No natural aging is allowed in Disneyland. Artificial materials were used so that they could be painted with the proper patina before opening day and touched up regularly so that they would always appear to embody imaginings. Like Mies's Farnsworth house, the constructions in Disneyland do not belong to the world of the everyday, but Disney's exist not in the realm of intellect but in that of Technicolor landscapes and cute singing rabbits. Everything must be artificial so that this more intense feeling of reality can be achieved.

The geography of Disneyland, in addition to being a clever way of exploiting and promoting the production of the Disney studios over the years, is also a pretty fair representation of the American consciousness during the Populuxe period. One enters on Main Street USA, an evocation of a friendly, happy, oddly familiar era and environment, though one that few visitors have actually experienced. Much of the point of Main Street was to allow a long view of the castle that terminates the street and serves as the central point and symbol of Disneyland. From the end of the street radiate the four lands which were made so familiar by the television program. There is Frontierland, which packaged the period's great concern with its history of migration and settlement in terms of the Hollywood version of the Old West. *Disneyland,* the television show, gave 1950s America its version of Davy Crockett and the coonskin cap. Tomorrowland represents the popular preoccupation with the future, which was synonymous with space travel. In the early years, there was a house of the future too, but that was eventually removed. Fantasyland is bedrock Disney, with reminders of the great animated movies that made his name a household word. The exotic Adventureland sums up Africa, South America and Southeast Asia as places of lush plants, large verandas, fierce animals and headhunters. It is a marvelous pastiche, but, unfortunately, it probably is an accurate reflection of the nation's view of what was to become known as the Third World. During the 1960s and 1970s, the United States fought a war in Adventureland.

The architect Charles Moore has called Disneyland a kind of symbolic downtown for Los Angeles, the pedestrian center it has never quite had. In this sense it was a precursor to what was to happen a few years later when metropolitan areas began developing cleaner, privately managed, better-maintained substitutes for downtown, first in suburban shopping malls and more recently within the city itself, in developments like Boston's Faneuil Hall Marketplace and Baltimore's Harborplace. James Rouse, the developer of both those projects and some of the pioneering suburban malls, has said that Disneyland inspired much of what he has done.

Interestingly, both Disney and Rouse claimed to be trying to recapture the sense of America they had developed growing up in a small town. Another great imagemaker of the Populuxe era, Norman Rockwell, chronicled a sunny, good-natured kind of small-town life. In fact, the small towns were dying. People were leaving the ones that were far outside metropolitan regions and moving to the ones that were near cities in such great numbers that these latter towns were turning into something else entirely. While Rockwell may have been painting his memories of Main Street, Disney enshrining it and Rouse starting to think about its replacement, the thing itself was doomed.

What was replacing Main Street was, of course, the strip, and it was during the Populuxe era that the strip was at its most raffish. It was on the way from somewhere to somewhere else, and it was, therefore, in terms of taste and image, a kind of everyman's no-man's-land. It was most often in the suburbs, but it could be anywhere along an arterial street or road. Los Angeles has long been a whole city made up of strips, although that quality is changing rapidly. The commercial strips of today are very different from the Populuxe commercial strips because today's are far more standardized—everywhere lined with outlets of the same handful of franchise giants, all built to more or less the same specifications. These designs tend to be more tasteful than the designs of the buildings along the Populuxe strip. They are certainly based on a great deal more research on efficiency and effectiveness than were the older strips, but they have a lot less quirkiness and personality. The strip was conceived just at the edge of respectability. Only very rarely did it offer beauty. Far more often there was humor. But always there was vitality.

The way to success along the commercial strip is to get recognized and accepted by customers who have very short attention spans because they are going at fairly high speed and cannot easily turn back. There had to be a sign, of course, but the building itself was important as a kind of secondary sign which verified the first. A sign might indicate a place to eat, but the building had to indicate cleanliness and liveliness, and it had to be clearly visible and recognizable in the vast, undefined spaces of roadsides and parking lots. A bit earlier, roadside businesses had often used naïve, pop-like symbols to get attention—a great plaster steer for a steakhouse, a big apple for a farm stand, a giant doughnut or a building shaped like a hamburger. Some of this held on during the Populuxe era, but the general trend was against such direct representation.

In fact, the commercial buildings of the Populuxe strip owed a tremendous amount to European modernism, in form if not in content. Like the pioneering commercial projects in Germany during the 1920s, especially those of Eric Mendelssohn, they often tended to be transparent, so that, at night, the interior illumination of the building would act as a beacon. Along the highway, this device had even more impact than it did in the city, where it was pioneered. And like Mendelssohn's projects, roadside architecture often took on very dynamic shapes, which echoed the sense of motion and probably carried the suggestion of speedy service besides.

The buildings on the strip were very cheap, virtually disposable buildings.

From the famous Strip in Las Vegas to the strip outside of town, commercial architecture was garish, lively, and cheap, designed to catch the eye of drivers speeding past.

They got their dynamism not from a sculptural look but from appliqué and inexpensive variations in framing. The single piece of high architecture that probably had the greatest impact on the commercial strip was the butterfly roof first used by Le Corbusier and popularized in this country by Marcel Breuer. This is a roof that sweeps upward from a point somewhere in the center. Le Corbusier used it to create a distinctive spatial sequence inside, but the highway drive-in restaurants used it for another reason. It increased the apparent size of the restaurant on the side facing traffic, which gave it a better chance to be seen and lure the traveler. It also gave opportunities for signs and other decorative elements within the acute-angled, jet age design vocabulary.

Frank Lloyd Wright had his impact on the roadside too, most often through the use of prowlike forms—dramatic cantilevers ending in very sharp angles—of the sort that appeared in much of his later work. There was also a genre of cocktail lounge–restaurant that would combine fieldstone walls with windows that tilted inward in a way that recalled details of his own desert retreat in Arizona. In one memorable standardized design, Phillips 66 service stations that appeared around the country during the early 1960s, the influence of Wright was combined with the international-style butterfly roof. The roof soared out from the office, and continued to ascend and narrow as it sheltered the gas pumps and came to a sharp point almost at the side of the road. There, the pole that held the main sign appeared to penetrate the roof, but was actually supporting it.

Many roadside buildings leaned slightly forward, with the same poised and eager stance of the cars of the period. Except for an overhang here, a tilt there, they were all more or less the same cheap and very small buildings. But they had to try very hard to look distinctive. The McDonald's arches—not the parabolic M, but the arches that reached around the entire stand—were truly a roadside inspiration. They transformed quite an ordinary little building into something boldly scaled and certainly memorable. There was a vague suggestion that these were structural, but nobody really cared whether they were or not. They did the job, which was making people notice.

A variety of roadside building that is almost extinct is the independently operated motel. Chains and standardization have put an end to the exoticism and ingenuity of buildings that were trying to lure traveling families in for the night. Although there had been motor cabins for as long as there were automobiles, the motel was largely a post–World War II phenomenon. The older tourist courts had suffered from a vaguely unsavory reputation, and as late as the 1950s, trade publications still spoke about the problem of lingering identification with gangster hideouts and "the hot sheet trade." But at the same time, industry surveys indicated that Americans, and especially women, greatly preferred motels to downtown hotels. Those surveyed complained that in downtown hotels they didn't know how to act, what to wear, how much to tip, while in motels everything was informal and predictable. From 1945 to 1963, only eight new hotels were built in American downtowns—except for Las Vegas and Miami Beach—while thousands of motels opened. They tended to be small, one- or two-story buildings of simple construction, but with signs and check-in offices that generally tried to combine the image of efficient modernity with the fun of being on vacation.

Most of these were doomed by the proliferation of the interstate highway network, which gave the great advantage to very large motels on expensive land near the interchanges. Those that do survive tend to be in resort areas, where the location is still good but the land is not so valuable and the business not so good that a larger building must be erected. Places like the Wildwoods, on the New Jersey shore, and Myrtle Beach, South Carolina, still have concentrations of Populuxe motels. They probably won't last much longer because these buildings, which were cheap to begin with, are showing their age badly and will probably be renovated in a fashion that appears more up-to-date. The Satellite Motel in Wildwood Crest, for example, is a museum piece today, but when it was conceived in the fifties it was the latest thing. It has all the Populuxe earmarks, beginning with an immense, asymmetrical cantilevered overhang that catches the eye and holds a sign. This connects to a huge gable, a blown-up version of the kind that was appearing on suburban houses and would later mark the standardized Shell stations. An enormous window is screened by a curtain of hanging metal balls, perhaps some subliminal atomic imagery. The lobby itself features a stylized map of the world, with a satellite superimposed, and it takes a page from Lapidus's work by having a grand stairway to nowhere in particular. The staircase provides an opportunity for the nicest touch of all, a simulated wrought-iron balustrade in a design that includes classic 1950s prickly-grapefruit satellites. This Satellite is unusual in taking its theme all the way to the doorways to the rooms. These are covered with siding that has been installed at an angle to give a sense of dynamism. The whole thing is a rather elaborate piece of space age folk art. (The Astronaut, just down the street, is not nearly so inspired.)

And one aspect of the Wildwood motelscape deserves special mention. Despite the towns' name, the three Wildwoods are on a barrier island that is naturally treeless. But all of the motel pools are lined with artificial trees, some of them palms with broad plastic leaves, most of them evergreens with "foliage" that seems better suited to cleaning commodes. Ugly and not the least bit arboreal, the pool trees of the Wildwoods dwell in the land of pure symbol.

The roadside motels and the popular resorts were created without the help or advice of serious architects, and in most cases there were no architects at all. Most serious architects paid little attention to the radically changing character of the American landscape. The advocates of European modernism had written celebrations of the car and the freedom of the road without once mentioning Big Boy drive-ins or Manny, Moe and Jack, and their American followers did not appear concerned that things weren't working out according to plan. Still less did they realize that the way in which people were responding to architecture itself was changing. Modernism had never aspired to be likable, merely universal. People would have to be educated to understand and appreciate it. That kept architects from noticing that, although pieces of modernism

INTRODUCING
AMERICA'S MOST SUMPTUOUS HOTEL
THE
Beverly Hilton

Synonymous with the gracious living of Beverly Hills, the magnificent new Beverly Hilton is the most recent member of the famous Hilton family of distinguished hotels. Ideally located at Wilshire and Santa Monica Boulevards, the hotel is of California contemporary style and has 450 air-conditioned rooms many with private balconies. Among the glamorous attractions are spacious landscaped grounds, sunken swimming pool, cabanas, shops and parking for 1000 cars. In keeping with friendly Hilton Hospitality, guests at this new hotel will enjoy the finest service, unexcelled food and the foremost in entertainment. The four restaurants and five cocktail lounges including L'Escoffier, The Bali Room and The Star On The Roof are each decorated in smart, distinctive decor.

Hilton Hotels
AROUND THE WORLD
CONRAD N. HILTON, PRESIDENT
EXECUTIVE OFFICES • THE CONRAD HILTON • CHICAGO 5, ILLINOIS

The Beverly Hilton, designed by Welton Beckett, was the first urban hotel built to accommodate cars. Other auto architecture: drive-in flying saucer and upside-down and golden arches; undulating canopy.

had been appropriated to sell hamburgers or mufflers, and a bit even let into the house, the straight stuff was nearly everybody's last choice. The architectural and emotional power of the traditional city was in question, and urban renewal just about killed it completely. And there was nothing to take its place. Americans had become accustomed to experiencing their surroundings in a way that was discontinuous, selective, drawn to the shiniest sign or the most persuasive symbol.

There were a few architects who understood this dilemma and sought to make buildings that had real emotional content. Inspired by the great Italian engineer Pier Luigi Nervi, several American architects saw the dramatic expression of structure, and the transformation of structure into sculpture, as the route to a satisfying modern architecture. This idea was first expounded, and demonstrated, by Matthew Nowicki in his State Fair and Exhibition Building in Raleigh, North Carolina, completed in 1953. The building's structure is hung from two enormous intersecting parabolic concrete arches whose tops are held aloft, at a 22-degree angle to the ground, by large steel columns. Nowicki died very young, before he had any other major commissions, but other architects quickly followed his lead.

In 1954, Minoru Yamasaki's massive concrete-vaulted air terminal opened at St. Louis and was immediately hailed as a model for a kind of building that was becoming increasingly important in American life. *Architectural Forum* noted that the vaulted interiors have a bit in common with those of New York's

St. Louis Airport, designed by Minoru Yamasaki, was hailed on its opening in 1954 as an air-age Grand Central Terminal.

Grand Central Terminal and mused that the new airport might be the Grand Central for the air age. Unlike the exterior of Grand Central, which seeks a weighty image of civic grandeur, the exterior of the St. Louis airport dramatizes the plasticity of the vaults. Also unlike Grand Central, which fit into the city, the airport, at least when it was new, stood apart from other buildings and sought to be a memorable shape in a vast empty vista. In this, it had more than a little bit in common with the less sophisticated architecture of the highway.

Nearly all of Yamasaki's work used structure in a way that was fundamentally ornamental. His characteristic buildings used concrete walls with vertical windows topped with pointed arches that have a vaguely Gothic look to them. His most famous building, the World Trade Center in New York, literally stretches this point for 110 stories. He was often criticized for trying to make his buildings into pleasant-looking packages, and that does seem to be exactly what he was doing. But in taking such an approach, he showed that he understood how people at the time were looking at buildings and what they expected of them. He was rewarded with many prestigious commissions, and his approach was so widely copied that there are dozens of Yamasaki-ish buildings around the country for every one that is the real thing.

In terms of personal fame, the star architect of the Populuxe period was Edward Durrell Stone, largely on the strength of two buildings most Americans had seen only in photographs—the U.S. Embassy at New Delhi and the U.S. Pavilion at the Brussels World's Fair of 1958. (Washington's Kennedy Center came later, largely the result of the fame of these two projects.) In 1937, Stone had helped design the Museum of Modern Art, a building that may have been mildly shocking when new but became a familiar fixture of New York. Stone's new buildings were not structural tours de force, but they were certainly not anonymous. They were packagelike buildings that seemed to float and shimmer in little reflecting pools and peek out from behind concrete lattice walls that brought pattern, shadow and texture to the whole composition. There were decorative glints of something goldish and lots of white marble. His strength was packaging the United States, and a lot of people found it very pleasing. Stone worked out similar themes, in humbler materials, in a Gulf gasoline station he delivered for Idlewild Airport. It worked pretty well there too, but one might have expected as much.

Idlewild was itself an embodiment of the Populuxe view of buildings and the landscape. Its design owes a lot more to the commercial strip than it does to Grand Central Terminal. The airport, which had hitherto been a single structure, here split apart into a series of buildings arranged along a loop road, without any sheltered pedestrian connection or rail link. The buildings within the complex included terminals for specific airlines and groups of airlines, a large international building and some ancillary facilities, including Protestant, Catholic and Jewish chapels placed near the automobile entrance to the airport complex but far from the terminals themselves. Like Levittown houses, the terminal buildings have sprouted many additions over the years, to keep up with growth and change, and the clarity of the architectural packages that

Jewish, Catholic, and Protestant chapels near the entrance of Idlewild (now Kennedy International) Airport.

were first created has been compromised. When it was new, Pan Am, for example, was clearly a disk-shaped building, covered with the signs of the zodiac. If you wanted to, you could see it as a large, rather corporate flying saucer. It was a memorable shape, and like buildings along a highway strip, each of the terminals was an advertisement that was trying to compete with its neighbors. There was little effort to add up to a whole place.

The most memorable building at Idlewild was the TWA terminal, designed by Eero Saarinen. This highly sculptural concrete building, with its soaring profile and dramatic interior, was immediately identified by the public as being "the one that looks like a bird." Saarinen, and even more emphatically his widow, strongly denied that it was meant to look like a bird, although they did say that it was intended as an abstraction of flight. Even today, when nearly anything goes in architecture, it would be embarrassing for an architect to make a building that looks like a bird. Still, consider that the plan of the building involved two soaring wings and its entrance comes up to what could be viewed as a beaklike point. If it has wings and looks like it's flying, then you can probably say it looks like a bird. Indeed, the thing that made it quite popular with the public, and a success for the airline as a promotional tool, if not as an air terminal, was its literalness. It had more in common with buildings along the highway that looked like hamburgers than it did with the very abstract international-style office and apartment towers that were being built in cities. And the interior, which featured a grand, somewhat art nouveau stairway with a bridge across the high entry space, and great curving spaces, was quite satisfying as well. Lapidus, admiring it, viewed it as a higher-class version of the effects he was trying to achieve.

Saarinen probably came closer than any other architect working at the time to reconciling the ideas and concerns of "serious" architecture with the realities and fantasies of the Populuxe environment. Just as his chairs were technologically innovative and designed for a contemporary American setting, Saarinen's buildings attempted to explore new forms to address contemporary concerns. Perhaps the most drastic of these was at Dulles Airport, another soaring though not remotely birdlike building, where Saarinen redefined the gate waiting area as a bus that would take passengers to their planes. Critics at the time admired this functional innovation tremendously, but many were uneasy with the frankly expressive and emotional nature of both airport buildings.

Unlike Mies, whose buildings were subtle variations of two patterns, Saarinen seemed to begin anew with each project. His first major commission, the General Motors Technical Center in Warren, Michigan, was outwardly Miesian, although it had some showy interior spaces, especially in the styling building, which was built for styling chief Harley Earl. And at the same time Saarinen was doing the sculptural airport buildings, he was designing some very modernist-appearing suburban buildings for IBM, whose design was extremely concerned with incorporating parking lots into the architecture. His CBS Building in New York was an aggressively massive and somber office tower, as un-Miesian as you can get, and his colleges at Yale were just short of picturesque. He faced the charge that his buildings were mere packages, each different from the others just for the sake of being different. This seems unfair. Saarinen's explorations of different approaches represented an acknowledgment that architecture did not have all the answers and that there was a lot to be learned from experimentation. But even if you concede that the buildings were just packages, that does not seem as damning now as it did then. The building as package reflects an understanding of the nature of the modern environment, which is fragmented physically, psychologically and perceptually. If buildings are perceived not as components of a particular place but simply as incidents along a highway or pictures in a magazine, they had better have an identifiable image, one to which people can respond emotionally.

Saarinen's architecture did have its impact along the highway. The sculptural, dynamic shapes of the two airport buildings and of his hockey rink at Yale were adapted to become porte cocheres for motels or rooflines of roadside restaurants. One of the more dramatic adaptations was Willow Grove Lanes in Willow Grove, Pennsylvania, which opened in 1961, and was for a long time the largest bowling alley in the United States. With 116 lanes, it represents the high-water mark of the bowling boom of the Populuxe period. Manufacturers of automatic pin-setting equipment succeeded in turning what had been a dark, masculine activity that smelled of stale beer and cigar smoke into a recreational activity for the entire family. Because bowling was seeking a new image, developers of bowling alleys tended to use the most up-to-date colors and decorative motifs. Nearly all the bowling alleys that survive today are virtual museums of Populuxe.

Eero Saarinen's TWA terminal at Idlewild, with its beak and two wings, reminded people of a bird. Inside, too, its spaces soared.

But Willow Grove is the ultimate. While other bowling alleys dramatized their dynamism by having their signs lean forward, Willow Grove uses the building itself as a sculptural element. Its main entrance is a massive, sweeping beak of turquoise-colored reinforced concrete, an inspiration that owed a lot to Saarinen. It is a lot more overreaching and a lot more awkward than anything Saarinen ever did, however. And while Saarinen's goal was always to have his buildings and furniture be "all one thing," the concrete expressionism of Willow Grove is only one of many elements in a multifaceted roadside fantasy. The building has the sculptural entrance and a swept-wing plan that celebrates the future, but it also embodies the accompanying suburban dream of rusticity. The building stands on what appears to be a fieldstone foundation, and the desks for renting lanes and shoes are made of local granite and schist. The overall effect, however, is not so much Pennsylvania countryside as the stone age suburbia of television's animated Flintstones. An outdoor pool with fountain near the main entrance strives for a show-business rural effect, and

Quite a bit of Saarinen, a little Wright, and a lot of other stuff was mixed together in the design of this huge bowling alley in Willow Grove, Pennsylvania. Right: The interior of the Tiki Room, the largest of the three restaurants in the complex.

the Waterfall Lounge, the bar that overlooks the pool, is expressed on the outside by a pointed wooden bay that recalls the work of Frank Lloyd Wright. There is also the Tiki Room, a murky exercise in the Pupu-Platter–Populuxe–Polynesian canned-pineapple-cooked-over-an-open-flame mode that was common in restaurants during the period. The interior of the building also includes wooden sculptures of an Indian and a rearing horse, to nail down the Frontierland market.

Sadly, the building is no longer operating as a bowling alley, and a huge regional shopping mall which is designed to evoke a turn-of-the-century amusement park has been built next door. The almost precariously soaring grand entrance to the building, embodying as it does an overwhelming faith in the future, appears an affront to the far more expensive exercise in nostalgia next door, and will probably be greatly altered or destroyed. It is a remnant of the awkward adolescence of the suburban culture, and it evokes uncomfortable memories. Its vulgarity is not yet old enough to be charming.

KODAK PAVILION

AMERICAN-ISRAEL PAVILION

The End of Populuxe?

The 1964 New York World's Fair should have been a Populuxe extravaganza. It had a Ferris wheel in the shape of a giant tire. Its centerpiece, the Unisphere, was a shiny metal rendition of that familiar futuristic image of the earth being orbited. The fair had towers that looked like flying saucers on sticks. In the Ford Pavilion, you could ride in a real convertible past a Disney version of the lives of cavemen and astronauts. Inside the General Motors Pavilion, which many people said looked like a giant tailfin, you could see a future that included underwater cities, complete with cute little family submarines, futuristic farming and cities with roads twice or three times the width of those that most of the visitors had driven in on. And at the General Electric Pavilion, you could stand in a space that seemed set up for some religious rite and stare at a dome beneath which a thermonuclear fusion reaction was simulated.

It opened on an April day on which a New York black activist had threatened to stall cars on all the access roads to the Flushing Meadows site. Even though the threat proved empty, the opening day crowds were sparse, because people stayed home to avoid the traffic. By 1964, previous futuristic promises to the contrary, Americans were well aware that bigger highways can also mean bigger traffic jams. And although the fair ended up with respectable

attendance figures, there was clearly not the kind of overwhelming enthusiasm for such a grand excursion into the future that might have been found only a few years before. The dreams of the future presented by General Motors were a little bit tired. They had been around for a while. People had seen them on television and in magazines. Americans seemed to be getting a bit jaded about the future; it had been around for too long a time. While the 1939 World's Fair had helped shape American culture, the 1964 fair was largely familiar, and was seen as, at most, a pleasant diversion.

It is the nature of styles to change, of course. Fashions, like flowers, give life color, but only because they bloom for a while, then die and give way to new, different beauties. The instantaneous communication and increasing sophistication of marketing during the Populuxe era quickened the pace of change and shortened the seasons of every kind of fashion. Populuxe was more than a single fashion; it was a cluster of attitudes and assumptions into which many fashions fitted. It was a new approach to fashion because it engaged not just a smart set but the entire mainstream of America. Populuxe was a way in which "the Affluent Society," as John Kenneth Galbraith's 1958 book termed America, adorned itself and understood itself. It was the shape of newness, the

The New York World's Fair's vision of the future was a bit tired. By 1964, even monorails were starting to look old-hat.

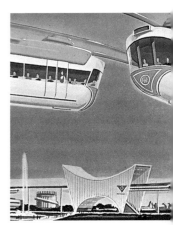

celebration of having made it. Americans were reaching for the promise of good education and a professional job for their children, and reaching for the moon at the same time. Often, the two seemed to be almost the same thing, and there was justifiable confidence that both could be achieved.

During the 1960s, Americans finally did see their countrymen land on the moon, and a great many of them sent their children off to college and a wholly different kind of life. For most, the promises of the Populuxe period were, more or less, fulfilled. Still, by 1964 it was becoming clear that the look—and the meaning—of things was starting to change. The imagery that had enlivened the previous decade had begun to look embarrassingly naïve and even empty. Pop artists had discovered it, and began to produce images that were, at once, familiar and accessible, but ultimately subversive. Once you become self-conscious about your fantasies, they can never again be quite so satisfying. And Populuxe had been around for what amounted to a generation. It had defined the material reward of those who had fought a world war, the pattern of adulthood and family life for the Depression-born generation and the total environment of most of the children of the baby boom. The World War II generation has never truly given up on Populuxe; it can still be seen in close to pure form in mobile-home retirement communities in Arizona and Florida. But the young parents moving toward middle age and the baby-boomers exploding into adolescence each demanded a new imagery for their lives.

Surely by 1964, the feeling of bland self-satisfaction with material comfort that had been so characteristic of the Populuxe period was gone. In 1959 Nixon could use a washing machine to symbolize America and it was a masterstroke, but in 1964 it would have been ridiculous. One reason was that people began to realize that there were a great many people in the country who could not even aspire to buy a washing machine. The crusade for black legal and economic equality, which had been fought out on the streets of southern cities and in the courts during the previous decade, finally penetrated the national consciousness. And although the American dream had seemed to be working so well, the great numbers of poor people that Michael Harrington's influential 1962 book had termed "the Other America" finally made a claim on the nation's conscience, at least for a time.

In its story on the opening of the 1964 World's Fair, *Life,* that perennial cheerleader for the future and celebrator of the promise of America, called the fair "all candy-bright and gay in a world that is in fact harsh." This was a drastic piece of revisionism, asserted with such casualness that whole hierarchies of editors must have assumed its truth. Although the World's Fair's planners could never have anticipated it, the fair came during a period of national atonement. Laws against discrimination were being passed, the nation had declared a "war on poverty," the rural poor of Appalachia evoked national compassion and public aid. It was recognized that the nation's cities had virtually been destroyed, and a national effort at large-scale urban renewal was launched.

The immediate cause for this flurry of lawmaking and guilt had happened only six months before the opening of the World's Fair. On November 22, 1963,

President Kennedy was shot in Dallas. Kennedy, who had so forcefully embodied the image of American activism and faith in the future, was suddenly gone, and the nation seemed to come to a stop to reflect on what it had been doing. Many of the anti-discrimination and anti-poverty laws that were passed during the aftermath of the assassination had been proposed, with little hope of passage, before he was shot. But the period of national penance, combined with President Lyndon B. Johnson's legislative genius, made them happen. The Kennedy assassination, followed quickly by the shooting of the chief suspect, Lee Harvey Oswald, on national television, gave Americans a new way of looking at their society. It had stopped being a place of infinite progress and ever-expanding promise. Instead, there were suspicions of dark and far-reaching conspiracies. There had been questioning during the late 1950s about whether Americans had lost sight of their "national purpose," and Kennedy's appeal had come, in part, from his promise to get the country back on track and in motion. But until the assassination, it had never before been suggested that America was a "sick society." Americans worried about all that shooting in the television Western programs and whether the country would be done in by a gunfighter mentality. Surely, the nation's confidence was shaken, and dealing with the present seemed far more urgent than dealing with the future.

Such questioning of the present and the future made two of the chief Populuxe motifs—futuristic speed and the pioneering spirit—somewhat problematical. The images of popular design are not intended to raise questions or doubts. To succeed, they must win barely conscious acceptance. The shooting of Kennedy was so deeply shocking that it changed the public consciousness virtually overnight. It was no longer possible to be truly innocent anymore.

Still, even if Kennedy had never been shot, there were plenty of indications that Populuxe was on the way out. Some of the social trends—increasing personal income, suburbanization—continued into the 1960s. Others, such as the baby boom, which peaked in 1959, had ended abruptly by 1963. In each case, the pace of the change had slowed, and the changes in people's lives no longer called for the kind of celebration that seemed necessary during the late 1950s. Suburbia had become so firmly identified as the heartland of the American people, the normal place to live, that it ceased to be either a utopia or a scandal. The hedonism that had characterized the Populuxe era continued, but it was consolidated, digested and expected. It no longer called for outrageous expression. The suburban building boom continued apace and houses continued to grow and grow. Automobiles remained large and added features that made them bigger gas guzzlers than ever. Expenditures on luxuries and entertainment increased, and the retailing industry exploded out of downtown and began to cover the landscape. Even after the Vietnam War became intense and inflation began to rise, the living patterns shaped by the automobile and the mass media continued to transform the American landscape. The issue of suburbanization had been settled. It had happened, and now a generation was reaching adulthood, or at least consuming age, who had never experienced living anywhere else.

Populuxe imagery was about movement, pioneering, change, the excitement of a leap into the unknown. It was a way of selling products, but it was also a way of helping people understand changes in their lives for which they could not possibly be prepared. "Never before" was a phrase that had real meaning in 1954, but by 1964 it was beginning to sound hollow. There kept on being more of everything. There were more kinds of appliances, more cars on the road, more roads, more houses, more products for all sorts of uses. But were they truly new and improved? There was cause for doubt. People had been caught in too many traffic jams to respond uncritically to the lure of the open road. People didn't stop buying automobiles, but they had become a necessity, not an achievement. They continued to buy houses in the suburbs, but they expected that too. The enormous changes in the shape and quality of the American environment continued, if anything, more rapidly than they had in the 1950s. But the pattern had been set, and people did not feel the need to dramatize the changes quite so vividly as they had before.

Someone who was able to buy a new car for the first time in 1955, 1956 or 1957 might have wanted tailfins, as a mark of having arrived. It was a moment for cars that could brag about themselves. Tailfins, because of both their association with the high-status Cadillac and the way in which they evoked jet age speed, were the perfect embodiment of that moment in the history of the consumer economy. The automobile industry was dependent on making people buy cars more often, however, and the next car did not need to express the same kind of fantasy. Ideally, it would say something else, something a bit more sophisticated and subtle. Tailfins were subjected to widespread criticism and scorn, even within the auto industry, starting in 1959, the year they reached their peak on nearly all models. They began to disappear in 1961, and by 1964 only the Cadillac, which had pioneered them sixteen years before, still had them. And by 1965 even the Cadillac's fins were reduced to vestigial

The reality of congestion had overwhelmed dreams of the open road, and cars' rear ends had turned almost sedate.

fender ridges, a far cry from the car's lethally sharp profile of six years earlier. Similarly, two-toning, which had dazzled the eye in the mid-1950s, was virtually non-existent by the early 1960s. Chrysler also phased out its double-boomerang "Forward Look" logo, which was too closely associated with tailfins and the nouveau riche look that had once saved the company.

And like the automobile, the characteristic object of the age, other aspects of the Populuxe environment experienced transformations into quiet respectability, even as their proliferation continued. Fast-food outlets along the highway began to be somewhat more domestic-appearing in their design and restrained in their signs. Many municipalities adopted ordinances to regulate the signs and the buildings along the strip, with an eye to creating a more dignified entrance to residential areas and maintaining property values. At the same time, many of the small-time operators began to be pushed out by big-time franchise operations, like Colonel Sanders and McDonald's. These could afford large-scale television advertising and architecture that was identifiable but not stridently attention-seeking. So these enterprises, which had been as raffish as the rest in their early years, saw greater profit and freedom of expansion in being perceived as good neighbors. During the mid-1960s, McDonald's golden arches disappeared, and people began to be allowed to sit inside. They were converted from drive-ins to restaurants for a family night out.

The early 1960s also brought the transformation of the shopping centers by the side of the road into enclosed malls. They were consciously designed to replace downtown and the small-town main street, and they accelerated the standardization of American shopping. The earlier roadside shopping centers tended to have an improvised, not very carefully finished look, a feeling of newness appropriate to the pioneer-minded suburbanites. Even the earliest enclosed malls, however, sought a look of totally integrated design and permanence. They incorporated churches and community rooms and sought to be new centers for the fragmented environment of suburbia. During the 1950s, the architect Victor Gruen had provided the intellectual basis for designing the automobile-based environment in a way that restored some of the satisfactions of the old pedestrian city. During the 1960s, Gruen got the opportunity to bring his ideas to partial fulfillment as designer of many of the pioneering malls. Some developers saw social benefit, and all saw profit, in leading people to identify with their malls, and in some places they succeeded so well that the malls have turned into place names. The first successful enclosed mall outside of Minnesota, which was considered to be a special case because of its climate, was Cherry Hill Mall in Delaware Township, New Jersey. One mark of the mall's success was that the township voted to rename itself, after the mall. The malls most often had names that suggested rusticity and closeness to nature. They featured fountains and ficus trees, not futurism.

On the home front, development housing became increasingly respectable, even for the relatively well-to-do. Earlier, houses had been aimed at a wide range of the middle class. Now, more luxurious housing was being provided for those who had been more successful than most—but were still used to a suburban living style—to move up to. Class distinctions had always been present in the suburbs, but the signals had often been difficult to read. By the 1960s people had been living in suburban areas long enough to figure out who was who and how things worked, and no new group was making the big move. Real estate advertising had moved from promotion of space and basic features of the house toward emphasis on snob appeal. "Your address will show you're a success" was an often-used slogan. Early in the Populuxe era, nearly any suburban address would show that, but by the 1960s it was important to be in the right development in the right part of the right suburb. The social upheaval of the first rush to the suburbs had cooled down. People had sorted themselves out, and if you were purchasing your third suburban house, it was difficult to feel like a pioneer.

And ultimately, Populuxe was limited by the same demographic phenomena that had brought it into being. As a commercial proposition, Populuxe was an approach to getting a generation that was small in number but high in per capita income to consume more than they needed in their houses, their appliances, their cars and all aspects of personal and family life. As early as 1953, *Fortune* had predicted major changes for the market in about 1965 as the first wave of the baby-boomers started to consume things. Actually, the change came a little earlier than that, because the clothing, record, fast-food and cosmetics industries succeeded in tapping into the baby-boom market early, and sixteen-year-olds were acquiring cars by 1962 and 1963 at a pace nobody would have dared predict a decade earlier. And while their parents had been

The First Family go to church on Easter Sunday 1963. American families identified with the Kennedys; when the President was shot the following November, suddenly everything seemed different.

The Populuxe era began with Elvis Presley—sexy, energetic, American. It ended with the Beatles—cute, ironic, foreign.

conditioned to look toward the future, anticipate it and plan for it, the baby-boomers took a very different signal from all that they had been exposed to while growing up. They were not waiting for the future. They *were* the future. The Mickey Mouse Club had told them daily that they were "the leaders of the twenty-first century," but who wanted to wait until fifty? Why not change everything at age seventeen? It was appropriate that the look of things, the feel of things, the prevailing myths and symbols should change with the coming of age of a generation that had been produced in greater numbers and raised with greater privilege, more expert advice and probably more anxiety than any before it.

Though many of the baby-boomers' parents once fought in wars halfway around the world, they were preoccupied with making homes that were safe and secure. The chief external concern was the Soviet Union, which seemed to be viewed more as a force of evil, and a test of American moral courage, than as another country. Although other countries were to experience their own postwar economic miracles after that of the United States, throughout the 1950s American material comfort and technological progress were unexcelled. It might be expected that a society in which a majority of people were frightened that they would embarrass themselves in hotels might be intimidated by Europeans and what was perceived as their greater refinement and savoir faire. A major part of Jacqueline Kennedy's success as First Lady was that she was as good as foreigners at their own game. She never had to worry about which fork to use. One wasn't sure about Mamie Eisenhower. When Jacqueline Kennedy traveled as First Lady, Americans could feel confident that she wouldn't make the kind of gaffes they feared they'd make themselves. But at the same time that Americans were intimidated by Europeans, they also condescended to them. The European role was to be charming, Old World and

just a little bit cute. They were Señor Wences, the Spanish ventriloquist on *The Ed Sullivan Show*, and Maurice Chevalier and a whole lot of self-possessed English butlers. They were nice, but not quite serious.

If the parental generation saw itself as a somewhat provincial and insecure but richly blessed people, their children were electronic cosmopolites. They grew up with television, which has the property of making everything seem equally near and familiar. All that they had seen made them jaded. And like children at any time, they had discovered what would drive their parents crazy. They had been brought up to believe that in consumption are both self-expression and power. And what they decided to buy was the Beatles. Today, the early Beatles, with their neat little suits and well-groomed though slightly longish hair, seem like the cutest foreigners of all, and they surely lacked the threatening, white-trash sexuality of Elvis Presley. The Beatles were an international youth phenomenon, and threatening for just that reason. Elvis had been tamed by being drafted into the Army, but the Beatles were extraterritorial. Parents saw, for the first time, the kind of cultural power their children wielded. They had, to be sure, fueled the Davy Crockett mania in 1955, when they were mere tykes, but with the Beatles they showed that they could reach out to any part of the world to find their enthusiasms. And the Beatles' own approach, which was a reinterpretation of American popular music, made the international ties all the stronger. The Beatles unleashed the entire "British invasion," which also included the Rolling Stones, a much scarier outfit.

The Beatles were part of a phenomenon by which British youth looked to America and the Continent, Europeans celebrated American rock and roll, and many spoke of an international nation of the young. In America, Beatlemania had a profound impact. Americans were not accustomed to invasions. Volkswagens and the pouty allure of Brigitte Bardot had their converts of course, but

The first Mustang is unveiled at the New York World's Fair, where it is greeted by a civil rights demonstration.

most preferred the more generous dimensions of the domestic product. In the realm of popular culture and material goods, if not of high art, America was used to being the influence on others, but not influenced itself. The idea of a British rock-and-roll group was almost as ridiculous as the idea of a Japanese car. Nevertheless, it happened. In embracing the Beatles, teenagers showed that the country was awakening from the American dream, into a world that was full of foreigners who could make a difference. And already, at the time of the Beatles' invasion, there were small groups of United States soldiers fighting in Vietnam, a place of which most Americans were only dimly aware.

But if Populuxe can be said to have come into its own during the auto-buying craze, triggered by tailfins, that began in late 1954, its end can be marked by yet another automotive frenzy. This was set off in April 1964, when Ford used the occasion of the World's Fair opening to unveil its new young person's "personal car." It was the Mustang, a sporty-looking, relatively inexpensive car that rapidly became one of the biggest overnight sensations in the history of the automobile. It was more affordable than the Thunderbird, by now turned bulky and boring, had ever been, and it came along just as the baby-boomers were reaching driving age. But though a significant number were bought for young people, most were driven by adults. The Mustang was perhaps the last thing that Americans of all generations really liked. Some dealers actually auctioned them off, because Ford was not able to make enough to keep up with the enormous demand. It was, in fact, a conventional American car, a four-seater, essentially the compact Falcon fitted out with a whole new body. And just as the 1955 Chevies allowed low-end buyers the fantasy of having a lithe cousin to the Cadillac, the Mustang was a light and lively T-bird for the masses. Earlier, the personal car had been a luxury, an American answer to European sports cars. The Mustang represented the arrival of a society in which every functioning adult had to have a car. It was an affirmation that this necessity could be turned into fun.

Thus, the arrival of the Mustang was well within the Populuxe pattern of abstracting the trappings of privilege and adding them to a basic product to be sold to the masses. No car since has had the cultural impact of the Mustang, because automakers no longer aim at a great mass market, but at more predictable specific markets. Surveys of consumer needs, desires and aspirations helped to create Populuxe, but the increased sophistication of those techniques helped lead to its demise. The assumption of advertisers that there was a mass market helped to create such a market and the idea that such mass consumption was a consequence of democracy. Advertisers have determined that the mass market is a myth, and in appealing to a large number of more specialized markets they have compromised the country's sense of social cohesiveness. But the Mustang, which was the enthusiasm of one Ford executive, Lee A. Iacocca, was the last successful bid by American car manufacturers for the affections of nearly everybody. In that sense, it can be said to be the last Populuxe car.

In appearance, however, it was very different from most of the creations of Populuxe, which involved endless elaboration and fantasy appliqué. Its look was, most of all, clean and direct. It was a bit of a throwback to the Fords and Studebakers of the early 1950s, cars that looked like cars, not airplanes or anything else. Although its design was unmistakably American, it did reflect the European idea that an automobile can be visually exciting by itself and need not resort to analogy. In fact, it did resort to one sort of analogy; it tried to look like a more technologically sophisticated automobile than it really was. Still, in purely visual terms, it is possible to see it as a departure from Populuxe and the beginning of something else.

The phenomena that seem to mark the end of Populuxe—the Mustang, the Kennedy assassination, the coming of age of the first wave of the baby boom, the end of American cultural dominance, the rise of the shopping mall, involvement in Vietnam—are a disparate lot. Many were a natural consequence of Populuxe, a carrying of ideas of the time to their logical conclusions. Populuxe grew out of extraordinary circumstances in economics, foreign relations and demographics that were bound to change. But the end was still shocking because rarely has an era strived so hard, in the midst of immense social change, to define the normal and the seemingly immutable. The Populuxe era confidently projected the American family—Mom, Dad, Junior and Sis—unchanged, centuries into the future, spinning through the galaxies in starbound station wagons. And today, Mom and Dad are divorced, the factory where Dad worked has moved to Taiwan, Sis is a corporate vice president, Junior is gay and Mom's a Moonie. The American Way of Life has shattered into a bewildering array of "lifestyles," which offer greater freedom but not the security that one is doing the normal thing.

The first manifesto of contemporary feminism, *The Feminine Mystique*, came out in 1963, and was a direct reaction to the Populuxe faith in salvation through spotless kitchens. Such faith may have been oppressive, but it probably died simply because the housebound woman became a luxury. Today, getting women out of the house and to work is no longer a matter of personal fulfillment but one of economic necessity. The economic pie has actually shrunk. Well-paid manufacturing jobs, which drove the economy, have disappeared in great numbers, and people have lost much of the social and economic ground they gained during the Populuxe era. The mass market is gone; many advertisers pursue the upscale and ignore the rest. It may be wrong to define democracy in terms of the things people can buy, but Americans tend to do so, and, by that measure, there is less democracy and less hope around now than when cars had fins.

So today, the objects of the Populuxe era have a certain poignancy and ironic force. Their optimism is charming and naïve, and they are valued today both for their innocence and for the way they point up what has been lost. At the time they were made, intellectuals decried them for being the products of a debased culture. But today, we tend to forget that criticism, or simply concede that ours is equally debased. In many respects, the intellectuals were probably right. America probably would have been better off if it had not become totally dependent on automobiles and if it had not obliterated much of its landscape in a kind of real estate development that keeps people apart rather than bringing them together. But it did happen, and we are living with the consequences. The fundamental changes that took place during the Populuxe period have their consequences in our everyday lives, and retrospective moralizing will make little difference.

It is equally foolish to be blindly nostalgic for the time. It represented a kind of cultural adolescence. The body changed. There were new responsibilities. You don't have to look very hard at that time of life to find the pain, the insecurities, the embarrassments that made it so very difficult. Today, some view the Populuxe era as paradise lost, but it was often experienced as purgatory with promise.

What the Populuxe era had, despite its preoccupation with the threat of nuclear annihilation, was a hunger for the future. Its visions of the future were often silly, but that's par for the course. What was important was getting on with it. "The future lies ahead," California governor Goodwin Knight liked to intone portentously, and comedian Mort Sahl made fun of him for saying so. Where else does it lie? Today, we are not so sure. We have become a ruminative society, gaining our nourishment from spitting up and chewing over pieces of the past. And now enough of the objects and the environment of Populuxe have been destroyed for us to value them. And they remind us that the future has a past, that it was anticipated with joy and impatience and that those cockeyed optimists were us.

ACKNOWLEDGMENTS

This book began nearly a decade ago with a telephone call from Mark Lofton, who was upset that a building we both hated was being remodeled. The turquoise and aluminum was being replaced with earth tones; the star motifs and the boomerangs were being painted out. The loss of a piece of what we had considered to be the bad taste of our childhoods upset us both.

Since then many others have contributed ideas, insights, and experience. Constance Rosenblum convinced me not only that there should be a name for this stuff, but that I might as well make it up. David Slovic introduced me to a wealth of visual material and had good suggestions. Alan Johnson and Woody Stange contributed superb photographs; Beth Sparre and Judith Sylk-Siegel checked the manuscript against their experience as Populuxe housewives; and Howard Shapiro perused my demographics.

An offhand remark by George Nelson helped spur my thinking and gave shape to the book, although there is little in here thathe would have approved of, and another casual remark, by Vincent Scully, took the architecture chapter into other directions. Living in the same city with Robert Venturi, Denise Scott Brown, and Steve Izenour has influenced me through the years. The book clearly owes much to the work of J. B. Jackson, Herbert Gans, and Reyner Banham.

My colleagues at the Philadelphia *Inquirer,* and especially Rebecca Klock, Stephan Salisbury, and William B. Collins, have heard far too much from me about this project and were still willing to offer advice. Jim Davis helped make it possible, as did Gene Roberts and Steve Lovelady, by deciding that I ought to write about architecture and design.

Otto Sperr nagged me to write a book. Roger Moss found me an agent, Barney Karpfinger, who understood the idea and helped shape it. I could not have hoped for a better editor than Martha Kaplan, who with tremendous intelligence and good humor has helped a novice author through what proved to be a complicated and messy project. Iris Weinstein knew what it should look like. And James Chan's contribution cannot be measured.

Index

A NOTE ON THE TYPE

This book was set in a digitized version of
the type face called Primer, designed by
Rudolph Ruzicka (1883–1978). Ruzicka was
earlier responsible for the design of Fairfield
and Fairfield Medium, faces whose virtues
have for some time been accorded wide
recognition.

The complete range of sizes of Primer was
first made available in 1954, although the
pilot of 12-point was ready as early as 1951.
The design of the face makes general refer-
ence to Century—long a serviceable type,
totally lacking in manner or frills of any
kind—but brilliantly corrects its character-
less quality.

Composed by Graphic Composition, Inc.,
Athens, Georgia
Separations, printing, and binding by
Toppan Printing Company, Tokyo, Japan

Back-of-jacket photograph courtesy of
H. Armstrong Roberts, Inc.

Designed by Iris Weinstein